THE RECRUIT BOOK

"Experience shows and research confirms that attracting the right talent is the most critical talent decision. This thoughtful and thorough book offers specific ideas and actions to make sure that the right people are recruited. The mindset, story, process, and technology for exceptional recruiting will help your organization become the employer of choice of employees your customers would chose."

Dave Ulrich
Rensis Likert Professor, Ross School of Business, University of Michigan
Partner, The RBL Group

"A must-read for anyone deeply engaged in sourcing the most valuable asset of any company: its people. This goes far beyond HR or People & Culture teams—it's essential reading for leaders at all levels, from managers and executives to business owners and entrepreneurs."

Kurt Sievers
Executive Director, President and CEO of NXP Semiconductors

"Hiring is the single most impactful leadership skill, yet so many get it wrong. In my 20+ years in big tech, I've seen how great hires can make or break teams, products, and even entire companies. The Recruitment Book is the essential guide for anyone looking to elevate their hiring game—whether you're a seasoned executive or just starting out. Barbara offers a fresh, insightful, and practical take on what truly makes recruitment successful."

Mahir Sahin
Senior Advisor, Alphabet Inc.

"The Recruitment Book is a must-read for anyone embarking on the recruitment journey, experienced or otherwise. With over 25 years' experience as client, supplier and coach, I still found invaluable insights and practical guidance, along with an engaging, curious, and playful approach that will resonate with many."

Rona Posselt
Founder & CEO, Firefly Partners, UK
(human capital consultancy for private equity and owner-managed businesses)

"Just as great stories convey emotion, so, too, do great companies. Barbara's innovative strategies, including a straightforward approach to uncovering your business's work aura, not only help to attract the right talent but also promise to save your most valuable commodity—your time."

Jody Robbins
President, Travels With Baggage Inc.

"Barbara understands very well that the right fit goes far beyond résumés and skillsets. This is why recruiting and retaining the right talent is an art rather than a methodology. A must-read for leaders who understand that great hiring shapes great companies."

Andreas Landgrebe
Managing Partner and Global Leader of Digital Transformation,
Boyden Global Executive Search

"I highly recommend this book to People & Culture professionals and HR managers! It delivers powerful insights that ignite meaningful discussions and inspire practical experimentation. Business partners—managers and investors alike—will find it compelling, as it speaks their language, while candidates will appreciate the unique way their perspective is highlighted. Most importantly, Barbara's writing is both personal and engaging, making The Recruitment Book a truly captivating read."

Armin Trost
Professor of Human Resource Management and
Dean of the Faculty of Business, Medical & Life Sciences, Furtwangen University

"What struck me about this book is the author's personal tone. Choosing the right workplace is a strategic decision that has a direct impact on professional and personal growth, well-being, and long-term career fulfillment. The right workplace is not just where you earn a living—it is where your purpose finds rhythm, your talents take root, and your spirit feels at home. This book offers a fresh perspective on how finding the right match is a defining choice for everyone involved."

Gisleine Silveira
Business Mentor, SCORE Mentors Miami Dade, Florida

BARBARA STAMPF

THE RECRUITMENT BOOK

Master the Essential Leadership Skill and ATTRACT the Best Team

Our mission at econcise publishing
is to create concise, approachable and affordable books
that help people grow and thrive in business and life.

If you're interested in staying informed about current developments in the field and getting more information about new books for smart learners, you are welcome to visit *www.econcise.com/newsletter* and subscribe to our newsletter.

This publication is subject to copyright.

All rights are reserved, whether the whole or parts of the material are concerned. This is specifically applicable to the rights of distribution, reprinting, translation, broadcasting, re-use of illustrations, reproduction by photocopying machines or similar means (including electronic means), and storage in data banks and data processing systems.

The use of registered names or trademarks in this publication does not imply (even in the absence of a specific statement) that such names are exempt from the relevant protective laws and regulations and are therefore free for general use. Product liability: Despite a thorough editing process, the publisher can give no guarantee for all the information in this book. Liability of the author or the publisher shall be excluded. econcise GmbH is not responsible for the content of third-party websites mentioned in this publication.

Cover image: iStock.com/jpfotograaf

Paperback ISBN: 978-3-903386-35-8
ePub ISBN: 978-3-903386-33-4
Kindle ISBN: 978-3-903386-34-1

First published 2025 by **econcise**
© 2025 econcise GmbH
Am Sonnengrund 14
A-9062 Moosburg (Austria)

www.econcise.com

Contents

Introduction 1

1 Recruitment comes in different shades 5
    Shade 1: Recruitment is a mindset 5
    Shade 2: Recruitment is buying and selling 12
    Shade 3: Recruitment is leading and coaching (in a surprisingly different way) 17
    Shade 4: Recruitment is investment 23

2 Recruitment tells a story 27
    The shriveled apple—and how stories influence behavior 27
    Have you got that certain something? 28
    How to find your certain something 34
    The three sides of a coin (and how to find that "certain something" in a company) 36

3 Recruitment is an "inside-out" job (or why employer branding should come last) 47
    From "outside-in" to "inside-out" 47
    The six key elements that stakeholders are looking for in your story 51
    Making an impact with your story 58

4 The process of recruiting the best team 65
    Step 1: Creating a need 67
    Step 2: Describing the job 67
    Steps 3 and 4: Describing the requirements and "magic moments" 69
    Step 5: Promoting the job 74
    Step 6: Screening candidates 76
    Steps 7 and 8: Interviewing and testing candidates 81
    Steps 9 and 10: Rejecting applicants and deciding for new employees 85
    Step 11: Negotiating with candidates 87
    Step 12: Onboarding 89

5 The role of technology: How AI can help you recruit the best team 91
    The intelligent use of AI in recruitment 93
    Using AI in the individual steps of the recruitment process 99

6 Recruitment is more than recruitment   103

    You can automate   104
    You can hire temporary staff   105
    You can upskill your team (educate from within)   107
    You can collaborate with others or outsource   108
    You can buy a team or company   109
    Find your own creative way to recruit your team   111

A concluding note   113

Endnotes   117
Index   120
About the author   123

For Lena and Ella.
May you find the right matches in your lives.

Introduction

Are you struggling to attract the top talent that can drive your business? Have you searched endlessly for the perfect fit for a particularly challenging role? Does it feel impossible to filter out the right professional or executive from a large pool of candidates for key areas of your business? Have you watched in frustration as top candidates slip through your fingers, forcing you to start the hiring process all over again? Has recruiting become more a source of stress and disappointment than a strategic advantage?

Whether you are an executive, a team leader, a recruiter, or a candidate, I wrote this book to make your life easier and to inspire you to look at recruiting through a fresh, colorful lens. My goal is to motivate you to explore new ideas and strategies for building a great team.

With 25 years of recruitment experience, I've helped tech companies grow by matching them with the right talent, partners, and investors. My focus has been on executive search, particularly for top managers, sales, and technical roles. I began my career in national and international human resources (HR) management roles with leading semiconductor companies Philips and NXP, where I played a leading role in scaling a new business segment across different ownership phases. Leveraging this background, I was also able to help build our family's ad tech company and lead it to a successful exit.

All of these experiences taught me one important lesson: that the right match is critical to a company's success. It is literally the beginning of everything. In this book, I want to help you make those right matches. I hope it will become a valuable companion for you, inspiring you with ideas and guiding you through your current and future hiring challenges.

You don't have to believe everything I say in this book. Instead, think of this book as a source of ideas to experiment with. Try a concept or two and see the results for yourself. After all, experimenting is at the heart of discovery. The results of your experiments may surprise you, and they may not be what you expected. But that's exactly how we grow and learn—by trying new things, reflecting on the results, and improving from there. That's how you'll get better and better at recruiting and finding the right match. I'd love to hear about your experiences—feel free to share your recruiting results with me at *office@barbara-stampf.at*.

One of my first bosses once told me that everything begins with hiring—whether it leads to a successful journey or a difficult one. At the time I thought he was exaggerating, but over the years I've come to understand what he meant. Getting it right the first time is a significant win for everyone and makes life easier for both the new employee and the company. I also realized that a successful journey begins when a new employee feels valued and recognized as an individual who can add real value. Finally, I realized that transparency is key in recruiting—when both parties are open about the positives and negatives, everyone knows where they stand and how to start the journey together. This foundation sets the stage for success.

Here's a quick overview of what you can expect in the six chapters of this book:

- Chapter 1 offers **fresh perspectives on recruiting** beyond a purely process-driven approach, with the goal of inspiring you to tackle your next recruiting challenge with a new mindset.

- Chapter 2 helps you **identify your business story**—exploring who you are and how you operate—as a foundation for attracting talented people and other key stakeholders. The goal is to reflect on and create an authentic narrative for yourself and your organization.
- Chapter 3 provides a **step-by-step approach to aligning your story with your stakeholders' needs and expectations**, and to highlighting and showcasing your company's uniqueness.
- Chapter 4 outlines the **key steps in the recruiting process**, emphasizing it as a means to deliver value to all stakeholders who have an interest in achieving the right match.
- Chapter 5 discusses the **role of technology in recruiting**, highlighting its potential as a collaborative partner in the process.
- Chapter 6 explores **different strategies for meeting your recruitment needs**, encouraging you to consider different approaches to achieve the right match.

If you're facing hiring challenges (as we all are), stay optimistic and don't give up, even when setbacks occur (as they often do). Recruiting takes practice, persistence, and a positive attitude. To borrow from a quote often (inaccurately) attributed to Winston Churchill, an optimist sees opportunity in every adversity, while a pessimist sees adversity in every opportunity. Learning is not a linear process; it's full of ups and downs, with each low ideally higher than the last. Success comes from resilience, like that of Diana Nyad, the US swimmer who, at age 64, successfully swam from Cuba to Florida on her fifth try—having first attempted it at age 28.

I truly wish this book not only helps you with your recruiting challenges but also inspires and perhaps even provokes you. If so, I've achieved more than I expected. If it makes an impact, I'd love to hear which thoughts, ideas, and concepts you found most valuable. If you have any points of criticism, I welcome them as well, as they can lead to fruitful discussions and further learning. (Just remember, along with the content, my heart is on the table for you—so please handle it with care.)

I wish you all the best in your recruiting and leadership endeavors, in both your professional and your private life. I am sure that with the right mindset, you'll make a difference—for your company as well as for the people you are recruiting. And remember, Rome wasn't built in a day: it took at least two. ;-)

May you make the right matches.

Warm regards
Barbara

Recruitment comes in different shades

Recruitment is much more than just a business function. It has many different facets, or "shades," which we are going to explore in this chapter. Each shade will give you a new perspective on recruitment and will encourage you to think about recruitment in a particular way. Understanding the different perspectives on recruitment will also give you the chance to reflect on your own recruiting practice.

The first shade is about the inner thoughts and beliefs that you're holding about recruitment, and how those thoughts direct you and become your reality. The second shade is about how recruitment can also be seen as buying talents and selling jobs, a culture, and dreams. The third shade focuses on the leadership and coaching aspects of recruitment, while the fourth explains why recruitment is also an investment.

Shade 1: Recruitment is a mindset

When you are thinking about the term "recruitment," what comes to your mind first?

When I was a young student, I first associated recruitment with the army—after all, that was where all the "recruits" were. When I studied Latin at school, I noticed that "to recruit," like its ancestor in an old French dialect, "recrute," has its roots in the Latin "recrescere," which means "to grow again"—in the sense of replenishing troops with new fighters.

It was only later that I realized that recruiting happens outside the army too—that every organization and company needs to recruit.

When I started to consciously observe how companies recruit, I sometimes felt like I was having a déjà-vu experience. There it was again, the army association, as I listened to people involved in recruiting talk about processes, structures, steps, and tools to find the right candidate. To my ears, it sounded exactly like I had imagined it would: adding new "fighters" to troops (or teams).

Of course, it makes sense for a company to have a solid recruiting process. But is it really the most important aspect of recruitment?

I also heard a lot of HR and business leaders talking about the needs and expectations of their organizations. Yes, that's important too, but maybe it's only half the battle.

Finally, when talking to applicants about their experiences in the recruitment process, I noticed that many of them seemed to be quite unhappy about the way they were treated in that process, especially when their own expectations were not adequately taken into consideration, when they didn't meet the company expectations, or when they just didn't feel valued as people or didn't get any helpful feedback (or got no feedback at all).

Despite these challenges, or perhaps because of them, I became more and more interested in how effective recruiting works, or could work. As a student, I also realized that one day I would have to go through such a process, and I wanted to be well prepared. At the time, I never imagined that recruiting, or "matchmaking" in a broader sense, would become a major part of my own profession.

Today, I can look back on more than 25 years of experience in international recruitment, primarily in the tech industry. And luckily, I have also gained a lot of additional experience from matchmaking and recruitment activities outside of my core job. That's the kind of experience in recruitment that you will most probably have too, experience that all of us are constantly and mainly unconsciously gathering throughout our lives: We are all recruiting without even realizing it. I would even claim that *we all recruit every day*.

Let me explain this in a bit more detail. Just think of your friends or favorite colleagues who you enjoy spending time with. You have literally "recruited" them into your life without even noticing that you were recruiting. Even if this thought seems a little strange for you, try to stay with it for a moment.

You are not alone in being surprised by such a thought, by the way. When I teach undergraduates at our local university, they usually believe they have never recruited in their life. I am used to getting strange looks when I tell them that they have probably recruited without realizing it.

When I then ask them what kind of values they look for in their closest friends, and what kind of characteristics their friends have in common, they suddenly start to understand that they have this underlying profile of an ideal companion in mind, and that they then match this ideal profile with people they meet throughout their life.

When we recruit friends, the matching process is usually intuitive. It's more like a feeling we get when we (unconsciously) compare our own value system with a potential best friend's value system, and when we (again unconsciously) conclude that this person's traits are the ones we look for in likable people.

If there's a match, we feel attracted to that person, and ideally, if there's a mutual match, the other person feels attracted to us as well. We want to know more about that person, we're curious, we want to see them more often, and we're happy to spend time with them.

Our final choice of lifelong friends is made over time based on how we perceive them to act on their values. We collect "evidence" about them, about our shared experiences, and about our relationship with them—the good times and the bad times we've had together. These experiences give us the opportunity to get to know each other well, which is a prerequisite for developing trust and building a very close relationship. We then reward this person, whom we will call "a friend," with lifelong companionship (and we usually get a lot back from them, too).

Can you grasp how you are recruiting friends? You compare values. You are engaged in a matching process—both intuitively and with the help of evidence. First impressions can make a difference, as can subsequent experiences as you get to know each other. You are curious about the other person's personality. You have a profile of an "ideal" friend or partner in mind. And your feelings play a role, too.

Of course, you are not consciously applying recruitment processes, tools, or matchmaking algorithms here (it might actually be a bit strange if you did so in your personal life), but it's all there—mutual expectations, making an assessment, a matching process, and ultimately the decision to let a person become a lifelong companion.

Any professional recruitment process involves both "soft" and "hard" factors. As with a recruitment process in our personal lives, "soft" factors include the personalities of the people involved, curiosity, feelings, values, interest in the other person, and personal attraction. "Hard" factors are the processes and tools used to identify, match, and evaluate the right person.

For effective recruitment, you will always need both soft and hard factors. You might have the perfect processes in place, but without considering the personalities of the candidates, you just won't be able to find the best people. After all, job candidates are first and foremost people, not processes, tools, or resources. And they prefer to work for great people, people who are able to use processes as a means to an end (in our case, successfully matching two parties) rather than as an end in itself.

No matter how well you have designed your recruitment process, great people will always have a feel for whether you are genuinely interested in them. They will notice whether you really care for them, and how important they are for you as human beings. They will see and feel your underlying values throughout the whole recruitment process or "candidate experience."

Do you enjoy meeting new candidates and finding the perfect "win-win" match between them and your team? Are you curious about other people—their energy, motives, and talents, as well as their successes and failures? Are you a "people magnet" yourself, someone others like to work with because they can feel how much you care? Are you able to create trustful relationships with other people? Do you challenge those around you in order to bring out the best in them? Or are you merely doing your job of recruiting another person and preferring to work with tools rather than people? Your first task as a recruiter is to be honest with yourself.

Where do you stand? How do you see recruitment? How full is your glass when it comes to thinking about recruiting? I probably won't be telling you anything new when I emphasize the importance of having the right mindset for effective recruiting (i.e., the thoughts and beliefs that you hold about *your role as a recruiter*). Having the right mindset is important in almost every area of our lives, whether we want to start a new business, lose weight, or run a marathon. And it's no different for your recruiting success.

How you think about recruitment will shape your behavior—how you will act as a recruiter. So before you start a recruiting assignment, I suggest you ask yourself a few questions. (Be brutally honest with yourself in answering them; you will also need that honesty in the recruiting process with the candidates.)

- Do you feel that you are being forced to recruit—perhaps because somebody just left and you have a vacancy in your team, because your market is exploding, or you just had to "say goodbye" to an underperformer?
- Do you see recruiting as a necessary evil that keeps you from developing products and services, managing your team, talking to customers or owners, or simply taking time away from your priority tasks?

- Are you primarily focused on recruiting processes (who needs to do what and when) and tools (from writing job profiles to using automated rejection emails)?
- Do you think primarily in terms of costs (e.g., how much time and money a recruiting process will cost)?
- Do you focus on the difficulties when you think about hiring (e.g., the difficult labor market situation in your particular domain—just imagine you need to hire a senior expert in cryptography or a CEO for an AI scaling challenge)?
- Do you see recruitment as sticking a band aid on the wound of an open position?
- Do you see recruiting as a task that is more suitable for your assistant than for you as a senior expert, team leader, or member of the top management?

If your first intuitive answers to these questions tend to be "yes," you're in a "glass is half empty" mindset when it comes to recruiting. In this case, I invite you to take a different approach to the recruitment challenge. After all, having the best people on your team is the foundation for your company's success in the marketplace, for creating great products, for building a great reputation, and even for convincing investors.[1]

Here's how you might take a different look at your recruiting task:

- You could see recruiting as a great opportunity to make your team even stronger. This is your unique chance to upskill your team—or at least to meet great new people.
- You could see recruiting as one of the most important tasks in your role as a leader or senior expert. Finding the right people could become the key differentiation opportunity for your company. With the right people on board, you will be able to do the right things ("first who, then what").

- If you are a CEO (Chief Executive Officer) you could view recruiting as a pillar of your core responsibility (you could redefine CEO as C=customers, E=employees, and O=owners and/or other stakeholders). Focus on "E" and find someone in your team to support you with the process side of recruitment. Try to put people before tasks.
- Recruitment could create opportunities that far outweigh the costs of finding the right person for the job.[2]
- If you truly care about people, chances are they will care about you and your business, too. Giving can be more important than taking.
- If you succeed in putting people before processes, you will be rewarded—both on the employee market and in your personal life.
- If you view recruiting as a strategic task rather than a tool, you also have the opportunity to make it one of your strategic differentiators. (If you outperform your strongest competitor in the talent market with a unique employer brand, that could be a powerful strategic move.)

As you may have noticed, this is a very different kind of attitude, a shift to a "glass is half full" approach to recruitment. In my opinion, that's the mindset of the winners in the recruitment market—and the mindset of people who live very happy and fulfilled lives.

Which recruitment mindset would you like to adopt?

DEVELOP YOUR RECRUITING SKILLS

Your recruitment mindset

Try to answer the following questions about your recruitment mindset:

1. Which of your current attitudes toward recruiting makes it difficult for you to move from a "glass is half empty" to a "glass is half full" mindset?
2. Are there areas in your life where you find it easier to apply a "glass is half full" mindset? What can you learn from these areas to apply this mindset in recruiting? (Be as specific as possible.)
3. Who do you know who is a "people magnet," a person who always manages to attract the best people to their team? What would you like to learn from this person? How can you begin to learn?

Shade 2: Recruitment is buying and selling

In most companies, suppliers and customers are handled by different departments—purchasing and sales. The job of the buyers in the purchasing department is to negotiate price, quality, and delivery time for the goods and services that the company needs in order to produce certain products or services. The job of salespeople is to sell those products or services to those who need them (who are then called "customers"), ideally repeatedly and at the best possible price.

The roles of purchasing and sales may seem too complex to be performed by a single organizational unit. But when you think about it, is the job of a salesperson (or sales manager) really that different from that of a buyer (or purchasing manager)?

Isn't purchasing, like selling, a lot about *finding and winning the right partners* (in the case of purchasing, the right suppliers)? Professional buyers are looking for partners who can add value, who are trustworthy, who are motivated to deliver their goods and services on time, at the right quality, and at the right price; partners with a win-win attitude, who believe in the end product, and who are committed to a long-term supplier–customer relationship.

And isn't it also necessary for a successful buyer or purchasing manager to sell their own company (and its values, spirit, products, financial outlook, and ecosystem) to the potential partner? Aren't they also responsible for attracting (*recruiting!*) the most suitable and reliable supplier—even more so in times of shortages of goods and services, such as in the aftermath of the Covid-19 pandemic? If you take a closer look, you will see that purchasing is not just a buying job. In fact, in involves *both buying and selling tasks*, part of which is recruiting the right partners as described above.

And what about salespeople and sales managers? Don't they also combine selling and buying? Of course, they typically have to "go out and find people" (customers) who have a need that they believe they can meet with their product or service. To do this, they need to understand their potential customers well, listen carefully, and then offer appropriate solutions—again, ideally at the right time, price, and place. (Does this sound familiar in the context of recruiting?)

This is the typical sales process, but what is the buying role of the salesperson? Well, if we take a closer look, we can see that great salespeople also "buy" (recruit) partners and their loyalty. They try to find the best customers—those who are a good fit for the company—and enter into a relationship with these customers, ideally a long-term one.

So in the end, on a meta level, it is about giving (selling) and taking (buying) for both functions—sales and purchasing. Both departments have the same goals: to find the right partners, offer the right solutions, and build a long-term relationship that makes life easier for both the supplier and the customer. And, as we've discovered, both functions also recruit.

Give and take—that's also the basic principle of recruiting. Recruiters sell. They sell dreams, an employer brand, hope, career options, and development opportunities. And recruiters also buy. They buy skills, experience, qualifications, talent, or potential. They also buy personalities. Recruiters unite both functions under one roof. They are both sellers and buyers, both sales and purchasing managers.

Have you ever considered hiring a purchasing or sales manager for one of your recruiting functions? Not many managers have, I suspect.

Commonly, recruiters are recruited among talented young people with an HR management education and experience in an HR role. But what if you can't find the right person with such a background? Maybe it's time to fish in a different pond. You could also approach HR recruitment from a different direction and hire people with completely different, but still very valuable, experience—for example in business functions such as sales and purchasing. Of course, you will probably need to motivate these people to move into HR, and of course they will need to bring the right soft skills with them—but chances are pretty high that excellent sellers or buyers will have such skills.

I am actually a fan of Dave Ulrich's philosophy that HR leaders (and I also see recruiters and recruitment managers as leaders in this sense) must have a good understanding of the business as well as a strong interest for people. They need to be both, what Ulrich calls "HR business partner" and "employee champions."[3]

From my teaching experience at different universities, I've received the impression that we tend to put too much emphasis solely on developing the skills for the employee champion role. Of course, empathy and showing care for people can be crucial for attracting the right people (see also "Shade 1" above). But these skills are of no value if you fail to understand the underlying logic of a business, including its business model, financial situation, and competitive landscape.

On the other hand, if recruiters see themselves primarily in a business partner role, focusing only on strategy, processes, and systems, they run the risk of neglecting the human dimension, which of course plays a key role in being effective in the matchmaking task.

In short, if you overemphasize just one of Dave Ulrich's roles (no matter which), you run the risk of either not attracting the right people or leading them in the wrong direction. How can recruiters help candidates take the next step in their careers if they do not understand their own business and its logic?

Dave Ulrich, along with Korn Ferry's Ellie Filler, also found that aside from the COO (the Chief Operating Officer, literally the "little CEO"), it's the Chief Human Resources Officer (CHRO) who has the most overlap with the CEO profile.[4] Both need a dual focus, ideally starting with their education, on business content and acumen as well as social, soft, and personal skills.

What I also observe is that graduates with an interest and a major in human resource management often find their first job in recruitment. However, if young graduates, who are likely to be inexperienced recruiters, do not understand that recruiting is like selling, this can only work well with (a) a top product (a great company, a healthy business, an admirable company culture, outstanding cooperation partners) and (b) a perfect understanding of the needs of the "applicant" (buyer).

From my own experience as a former young, inexperienced graduate in this field as well as from working with inexperienced recruitment managers in a range of different companies, I believe that young graduate recruiters only fully succeed if they are very reflective and able to respect their limitations while trying to hire more experienced candidates and coach them on the next steps in their career. It also helps if they are streetwise, understand the industry well, and have a lot of general knowledge beyond business.

When you use recruiters without such skills, you might run the serious risk of not being attractive for more experienced candidates at the first contact point with your company. In times of talent shortage, and bearing in mind the value of team diversity for creating better outcomes, this is probably not the very best idea.

DEVELOP YOUR RECRUITING SKILLS

Your role as a "seller" and a "buyer"

Try to answer the following questions about your role as a "seller" and a "buyer":

1. In what ways do you view your role as a recruiter similar to that of a salesperson or buyer?
2. What types of people are employed in the recruiting function in your organization?
3. How could you and your team profit from applying a "recruitment is buying" and a "recruitment is selling" perspective?

Shade 3: Recruitment is leading and coaching (in a surprisingly different way)

Let's look at recruiting from another perspective. As we've seen, it involves both buying and selling, but we can also see it as a leadership and coaching process.

Let me define leadership here as a process in which one party (the "leader") aligns their meaningful goals based on moral values with another party (the "follower" or "followers"), and where both parties are motivated (or motivate each other) to do their very best to achieve those goals (together).

Coaching, as I see it, is about being a "buddy" who asks questions and offers support along with a sincere interest in helping another person achieve a self-defined outcome. It is a bit like being a true friend:

- a friend with no self-interest, only an interest in seeing you thrive, grow, and be happy;
- a friend who asks and listens with neutral curiosity (playing the "Swiss neutral" role);
- a friend who also dares to ask the questions that have until now remained unasked, that will take you into uncharted territory beyond your comfort zone;
- a friend who supports you with unconditional motivation and trust. (It seems that in times of population growth, the anonymity of big cities, individualism, and the dominance of social media, the lack of true friends in the personal environment has led to an increased need for mentors, coaches, and even psychotherapists in the professional environment.)

"But how does any of this relate to recruiting?" you are absolutely right to ask.

To answer this question, let us start at the top: What is the primary goal of a top executive? "To be successful in business for the long term or forever," Simon Sinek might argue.[5] "To achieve ambitious goals set for the company," someone else might say. "To be happy themselves," I would add. So, implicitly, if you look closely, when top managers call for additional people to grow or scale the business they are trying to pursue and achieve long-term aims. They are looking for people who have the right experience, skills, and motivation to help them achieve ambitious business goals.

So far, so good. But the whole equation will only work if one "little detail" is fulfilled—and this is where true leadership (as defined above) comes into play. That "little detail" is that our top leaders will only be able to reach their ambitious goals when their business targets are aligned with the personal dreams and values of the new recruits. There needs to be a balance of buying and selling—the give and take described earlier in "Shade 2."

Let me give you a couple of examples. First, consider a company that is very focused on making millions and rewarding its employees with stock, bonuses, and generous salaries. I am not saying that this should always be the primary goal, nor am I criticizing it—after all, making money is one of the primary outcomes of business—but there are certainly companies where money is more important than in others. In such an environment, you need people who are also very money-oriented.

To take a second example, if a company is focused on growing and scaling through the development and creation of new products and services, it would be a much better fit for people who are growers, creators, and developers themselves—people who love to evolve, and people who are interested in the learning journey itself as much as the outcome.

If you have a business that is under stress—and that's example number 3—you need people who love to bring things to order, who thrive in troubled waters, and who feel positively challenged and motivated in times of change. These are people who thrive when the going gets rough, and who would not even mind jumping ship when the company is back on a profitable course.

So, as we can see, different people and personalities are needed in different business scenarios. Different situations and challenges that businesses may face—whether it is squeezing millions out of a business, following a learning and development path, or turning the ship around—require different personal values and skills to be met and matched.

At the beginning of one of my university courses, a master's student once asked me to describe the essence of leadership in three seconds. At first I was puzzled by this request, but then I decided to accept the challenge. Forced to reduce my answer to the single most important bullet point, I said: "Leadership is about aligning the business needs (or goals or dreams) with the personal needs (or goals or dreams) of the people who work for the business, and resolving issues between the two needs during the joint journey." I am not sure if the three-second goal was perfectly met, but at least I gave it a try.

When I gave this answer, there were a few moments of silence in the class, which is usually a good sign that students are digesting a message. The student who had asked me looked a little confused. I could tell that he was touched by what I had said, but then he said impulsively: "It seems that this lecture will be important for me, because it is also about me! In my previous jobs, I never experienced leadership being about me, but now I am very curious to learn more about this kind of leadership."

I had sensed that the original intention behind the student's question was not pure interest. It was more about putting me on the spot as a lecturer, as he admitted when I brought it up. He said he had learned from a Silicon Valley entrepreneur that if you can't explain the essence of a business topic in a few seconds, you don't really understand it. He actually tried this with every lecturer in his program, and I was lucky enough to meet his expectations.

At the same time, I was able to achieve my own goal of getting the students excited about learning more about leadership, piquing their curiosity, and creating an environment where everyone in the classroom was willing to listen, share their thoughts, experiment, and learn a lot. For this class, our goals were perfectly aligned.[6]

If leadership means aligning business goals with people's personal goals and resolving conflicts between them, then coaching becomes an indispensable tool. It helps create that alignment—beginning at the very first touchpoint: recruitment.

Remember that coaching is fundamentally about helping another person achieve their own goals, and the primary means of doing this is through a goal-oriented questioning approach.

A candidate who is primarily money-oriented (as in the first example above) will need questions such as

- How much money would you need to be satisfied?
- If you don't get a stretch bonus, what does that do to your motivation?
- What would keep you from running for your bonus?
- What makes you happy in life besides results (like money)? *(This encourages the candidate to open up about different life expectancies.)*
- Has there ever been a situation where you had to stop following your bonus plan?
- Camaraderie and bonus incentive—do the two go together for you?
- How do you feel about the prospect of making money with this team, product, service, etc.?

A candidate who sees themselves as a "grower," to take another example, would need questions about development and growth, such as:

- In two years' time, what would you like to have learned?
- What makes you happy about growing?

- What are your most important values in life?
- What role do results (and money) play for you? *(This encourages the candidate to talk about motives other than growth.)*
- How important is learning new content and behaviors for you?
- What are the last skills you learned? And where did you use them?

Ideally, you will always want to learn more about the candidate's values, perspectives, opinions, and experiences, with a genuine interest in learning more about their motivations. This will enable you to assess the degree of alignment between the candidate's personal values and the values of the organization for which you are recruiting.

This will also require a set of personal qualities and attitudes on the part of the recruiter (or leader), namely honesty, empathy (including a sincere interest in other people), curiosity, and a strong solution orientation.

Let's take a closer look at these essential qualities for a successful "recruiting leader," to wrap up Shade 3:

- **Honesty:** Let's take the example of a (strong) candidate who prefers to work in a stable environment. A great coach in recruitment, in my eyes, will support this candidate in choosing another employer who offers more stability than the coach's company can offer, knowing that this will be the better fit for the candidate in the long run. Does that seem too generous and candidate-centric for you? Well, it's actually a good mix of generosity and selfishness. I'm talking about being honest about what it will be like to work for the company you're recruiting for. In this particular case, that means honestly addressing how much stability a candidate can expect in your company compared to others (from a bird's eye view, so to speak). You can then honestly address other criteria (beyond stability) that will help the candidate evaluate your company versus others. So it's really about managing expectations in an open way. That's how you build trust, and then the candidate can decide for themselves if it's really a stable work environment that matters to them—or if the trust you've built up in your discussion could actually become a form of stability that they might also find attractive.

- **Empathy:** This is what I'd call "feeling for other people," even between the lines. It also includes the ability to recognize or "sense" what the candidate has not mentioned, what is said but may not be meant, or what exactly someone means when they say something (e.g., when a candidate says they are "looking for stability"). Empathy is a good basis for asking the right questions (as described above). For example, if a candidate emphasizes how much they value stability in a company, you might ask questions such as "Why is this important to you?", "How would you describe stability?", or "What are your fears if there is less stability?"

- **Curiosity:** What I mean here is having an open mind when exploring other people's expectations, their personal qualities, and their dreams for the future. It is this kind of positive experimental attitude that children have, a hunger to learn more about others (and about themselves), ideally without prejudice.

- **Solution orientation:** This is about having the energy to keep looking for the best solution—the one that works best for everyone involved—and always trying to produce the best possible results and outcomes. That could also be finding or creating a job for an excellent candidate who has applied for another job. In this way, solution orientation can be an invitation to the candidate to co-create a job that is needed in the company and attractive to the candidate. Honesty, empathy and curiosity will also help you find the best solution.

DEVELOP YOUR RECRUITING SKILLS

Your role as a "leader" and "coach" in recruitment

Try to answer the following questions about your role as a "leader" and "coach":

1. Think of an example where your leadership style (in recruiting) was strongly focused on achieving only your own goal, and you were not happy with the outcome. How could you involve the other person in formulating a common goal? What opportunities would it open up if you came up with this common goal?
2. Think about the leaders you have worked for. Which of the qualities described above (and what other qualities) did they possess and use? Where were they successful in recruiting, leading, and engaging people? What could you learn from them?

Shade 4: Recruitment is investment

"It is more blessed to give than to receive." This quote is to be found in the Bible, but we find a similar situation in the recruiting process, too.

Recruitment can also be compared to an investment. You have to put some money on the table before you get any dividends or interest. In my experience, the same is true with people and relationships. Whether you invest passion, time, or money, it will usually come back to you with an interest rate (again, in whatever currency—passion, time, or money). When you invest in a business, you do so with the belief that the investment will yield some (financial) benefit in the future. Likewise, you should have the same kind of belief and trust in the people you work with—and invest in them as well. So make sure you only hire people you believe in, and never hire someone with whom you haven't built a foundation of trust. When you believe in someone, you invest in them. Trust follows, and challenges become easier to overcome.

Manfred Winterheller, one of my mentors as a university teacher, later as a boss, then as a motivational coach, once introduced me to a simple yet powerful principle: The more confidence you have in yourself, the smaller the "net problem" you have to solve (see Figure 1.1). I would extend this idea further—your belief in others also influences the size of the net problem.

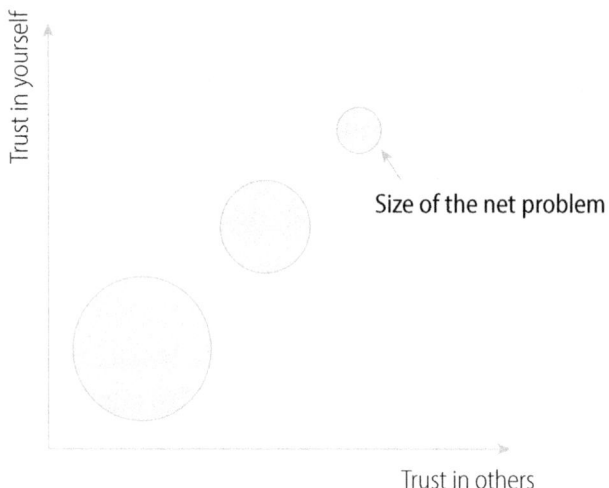

Figure 1.1 The size of the net problem decreases as trust in yourself and others increases

So if there's a net problem, what's the gross problem? It's the problem as you initially perceive it, with all its difficulties and complexities. But when you have confidence in yourself, you let go of the worries in your mind. This triggers the release of positive hormones such as serotonin and dopamine. As a result, you immediately begin to address the challenges, and what once seemed overwhelming (the "gross problem") now seems more manageable (as the resulting "net problem"). Conversely, the problem grows larger as your time and energy are absorbed by worry and anxiety. And this can be felt by others.

Just as others can feel when you radiate positive energy, they can also sense when you do not believe in yourself and others. They can sense your fears, and then both you and your communication partners become more insecure. Unfortunately, our brains are wired to focus on fears and "what ifs" rather than constant solution orientation. This works not only for other people but also for yourself. When you trust yourself, surprising results seem to follow. This is true for founders and CEOs as well as for students and parents.[7]

When people feel that you trust and believe in them, you also increase the likelihood that they will deliver better results, because they will feel that their net problem is getting smaller. Call it a self-fulfilling prophecy, the Pygmalion Effect, or a growth mindset. In their groundbreaking experiment, Robert Rosenthal and Lenore F. Jacobson showed how a teacher's preconceived positive opinion of a student can strongly influence that student's academic performance.[8] The researchers observed that when teachers believe a student is excellent, they consciously or unconsciously engage in highly demanding and supportive behaviors that contribute to that student's outstanding performance. (Recent studies by Stanford professor Carol Dweck and her colleagues point in a similar direction, finding that a teacher's mindset can significantly influence their students' growth mindset, which in turn can lead to higher achievement.)[9]

In a leadership context, demonstrating appreciative and caring behaviors has also been recognized as an important factor in positively influencing the performance of team members. These effects were observed as early as the 1930s in the famous Hawthorne experiments at Western Electric's Hawthorne factories where researchers experimented with different lighting conditions for workers and found that the mere fact that someone cared about the working conditions had a positive motivational (and ultimately performance-enhancing) effect on the workers.

You may have noticed it yourself—when you feel that someone really cares about you as a person, you are more likely to give your best. As Melissa Houston titled her recent Forbes article: "The art of caring leadership in business can increase ROI."[10] And the same is true for the art of caring recruitment.

If you want new people to tackle and solve tough challenges for you, invest in them first! Believe in their excellence, show the candidates how much you care about them. Invest enough first and you will reap the benefits once they are hired. You don't have to take my word for it—approach it like a scientist. Try it, observe the results, and then decide for yourself.

DEVELOP YOUR RECRUITING SKILLS

Recruitment is investment: The role of trust

Try to answer the following questions about viewing recruitment as an investment:

1. Have you ever hired someone you didn't fully believe in? Why did you make that decision? What was your inner dialogue at the time? What was the outcome, and what lessons do you take from the experience?

2. When you hire someone you fully trust, what thoughts and feelings go through your mind? How does your inner dialogue change?

3. What needs to happen during the recruitment process for you to place full trust in your chosen candidate?

Recruitment tells a story

After exploring different perspectives on recruitment in the first chapter, in this chapter I focus on the power of storytelling and how you can use it to attract the right talent to your team. I will first share how I personally discovered the power of stories, followed by an in-depth exploration of six key "story questions" that can help you uncover the essence of your own or your company's unique story.

The shriveled apple—and how stories influence behavior

Ever since I was little, I have loved being told stories. And when I was a young kid, I especially loved eating fruit while being told stories. What I did not like were old apples: Their shriveled skin put me off.

My grandfather Lois was a particularly gifted storyteller. I remember him telling stories about what had happened to him as a young boy, both the good and the bad stuff. His stories were always exciting, they could also be horrible or dangerous—and many of them touched my heart. I was thrilled by all his adventures as well as I was shocked by the hardships that he had to experience in his youth. And I felt so involved, and wished I could step in and bring the story to a Hollywood ending.

I became so captivated by the stories that I even forgot my dislike for shriveled apples. My grandfather would take a shriveled apple, cut it in half, and scrape out the flesh with a knife. Feeding me directly from the blade, which felt like an adventure in itself, he would tell me gripping tales—like the time he hid in a dark cave for days without food, or when his colleagues, teasing him for his fear of flying, pretended to shut down their plane's engines. As I licked the apple's flesh from the knife, savoring a taste I would never have sought out on my own, I was fully immersed in both the story and the moment.

Whenever I visited my grandparents, I kept asking for the "scraped apple," because in my mind and heart there was now a strong connection between Grandpa's amazing stories and the shriveled apple. I hoped that when I got my "scraped apple," I would also get another story.

Looking back, I think that the combination of stories and knife feeding might have been just a trick of my grandparents to get me to eat shriveled apples (my grandparents, who had lived through a long war and suffered from hunger, would never have thrown away food). But even if that was the case, I really loved that trick.

Have you got that certain something?

Great stories create emotion, and they evoke a hunger for more. They can make you want to try, learn, and like new things (maybe even shriveled apples). So they can really change your behavior.

But how does all this relate to recruiting?

Since the term "employer branding" was first introduced by Tim Ambler and Simon Barrow in the 1990s, it has become clear that if you want to attract and retain great people, you need to identify that special "something" you offer as an employer, a unique feature that makes you stand out from the crowd. Ideally, people will love to hear about that "something"—which means they will love to hear your story. At its best, it's a story that people want to be a part of, a story that makes them want to join you.

But what is that "certain something" that sets your company apart from the rest? It should be a combination of the following:

- Something that you stand for as a company or a team that creates a particular product or service.
- Something that is instantly recognizable both to people inside the company and to the relevant outside world—your key stakeholders and anyone you want to collaborate with. By recognizable, I mean something of which your own people can say, "Oh wow, yes, that's definitely us!"
- Something that evokes pride and emotion, and is truly authentic. You know it is truly authentic when people voluntarily share that "something" in their communities and with their friends without being told to do so.
- Something people want to hold onto, that they feel compelled to connect their own personal stories to, and that inspires them to try new things.
- Something so distinctive that even grandparents who read about it in the newspaper will want to tell their grandchildren about it (this could be a very special recommendation for a company that has an unparalleled level of trust).

Does it sound difficult for you to identify that "something" for your company as an employer? I don't think it really is. Just as every person is different, every company is different. Those differences do not have to be very big. Sometimes small differences can have a big impact on people looking for work opportunities. The little things count at least as much as the big things when it comes to creating a special "work aura" in your company. It's similar in our personal lives, isn't it? It is the little things, if we are ready to see them, that create real impact.

This special "work aura" is an imprint of the employer's soul, the energy that can be felt, seen, and experienced in the company, even from the outside. The aura is created by the sum of all team members and external partners. That is, all those who work in your company, and all those who are involved in the creation of your company's products and services. This includes their negative emotions (anger, fear, frustration) as well as their positive emotions, their health and fitness levels, and the way they approach problems and live their lives.

The first step to be able to understand or read the "aura" of an employer is to be attentive, honest, and clear about who you are as a company and who you are as a leader—and who you are not.

Founders and managers of smaller companies, especially start-ups and sometimes even scale-ups, often worry that they don't yet have a story to tell or that it's difficult to pinpoint a unique identity. However, if you've just founded a company, consider your own journey as a founder, the stories of your first employees, and those of your customers and leaders—their values, ideas, and dreams—as a starting point.

Entrepreneurship has become a trendy topic, especially among young people, so once you have a story there are many channels through which you can share it. Social networks (from LinkedIn to TikTok), your own website, but also the online communication channels provided by partners (e.g., investors, banks, sponsors, or funding agencies) are all great options. Additionally, founder garages, universities, coworking spaces, startup events like "Fuckup Nights," incubators, and local government initiatives provide excellent opportunities to spread your story.

Whether you are a startup, an SME, or a multinational corporation, it is important to identify that "something"—your uniqueness—which will then form the basis of the story that will help you attract the best people to your company.

How to find your certain something

In my opinion, the best place to start is to discover that "something" in your personal story (or personal brand). Most companies are unique because of the uniqueness of the people who run them or work for them. We could also compare them to a "baby" (the company) that inherits certain characteristics from its parents (the company's founders, leaders, or first employees). After all, companies always start with people—or do you know of a company that was started by a machine or AI (well, maybe that's still coming)?

The approach of starting with discovering your personal story is a bit like preparing an interview with yourself. Of course, you could also invite a friend or colleague to interview you, in which case I would still recommend thinking about possible answers to a few questions first.

The following questions can help you identify your "uniqueness," the core of your personal story. Answer these questions first, and then try to summarize what makes you unique.

1. What are your core values? (Write down at least five.)
2. What is special/unique about you that other people may or may not notice? What do other people say is special about you?
3. What have been the key events in your life that have shaped you? How do these key events influence your behavior (and maybe even your values)?
4. What is your purpose on earth? What are you here for? What mission do you want to accomplish in your lifetime? Why do you do what you do in life?
5. Where are you going in your life from today? And with whom? *(Next to "Who are you?" these are the central questions of life in my eyes.)*
6. What is the joy—and what is the risk—of being or working with you?

When you have honestly answered these questions—which may take some time—try to write down in a few bullet points what that "something" is that other people can expect from you. When you have your key takeaways in bullet points, you can tell your story to different stakeholders in different ways.

Let me give you two concrete examples of how this can work in practice, one about me as a person and one about Snigel (*snigel.com*), a technology company I've been involved with since its inception.

If you were to ask me the above questions, I would tell you the following story about myself:

Question 1: What are your core values?

My core values are:

- Health, nature, family and friends
- Honesty and freedom
- Ambition and results
- Cooperation and joy
- Solution orientation and making things better
- Learning and innovation

Question 2: What is special/unique about you that other people may or may not notice? What do other people say is special about you?

- My energy and passion that I put into most of the things I do.
- My reliability and loyalty, the honest words and passion in my relationships. I walk the talk.
- My smiling and sunny attitude, even when I have to solve very challenging tasks.
- The hunger to grow, to learn, and to try out new things. I want to create new wins every day and enable others to learn, grow, succeed, and be happy. I see myself as an enabler for others (and for myself).
- If you met me in a bar, I would not have to tell you anything about my enthusiasm—you would see and feel it.

Question 3: What have been the key events in your life that have shaped you up to this moment? How do these key events influence your behavior (and maybe even your values)?

I grew up in a traditional local business, a bakery. I was shaped by freedom, nature, my family and friends, the willingness to take risks and seize opportunities, and the experience of working together as a family or team.

My parents gave me a lot of freedom. They expected me to be able to deliver results independently, and they always said what they thought (from head-to-head to heart-to-heart communication). They also encouraged me early on to reflect on certain behaviors.

At school I had an excellent teacher who awakened my interest in people from different cultures and motivated me to go on an international exchange at an early age.

In my teenage years, I was plagued by a skin disease that had a great impact on me. It shattered my self-confidence and made me more humble (perhaps one of the reasons why I prefer to be backstage, supporting others on stage).

I have a close-knit, loyal group of friends I've made throughout school, university, and my later professional life. They've supported me along the way, always being open to collaboration, engaging in deep discussions, and helping me learn while supporting others in their lives. Helping and empowering others has also become a source of energy and joy for me.

Working in tech companies where brutal openness was the norm was not always a pleasure, but it was a great learning experience.

My husband has always given me the freedom, trust, and support to be who I want to be without any expectations of me. My two beautiful daughters are unique teachers and continue to ask deep questions about life. They challenge my beliefs almost daily and keep me focused on the here and now, especially with heated discussions during their adolescent years.

A near-death experience during the birth of my first daughter has left me with a bit of a health trauma, as well as a lot of hope and gratitude (and again, a considerable amount of humility).

Most of the time I was really lucky to have great people around me. It also taught me that sometimes you underestimate the luck on your way.

Of course, I could go on and on—I have lived on this beautiful earth for quite a few years now—but I think you already get the point of this exercise.

Question 4: What is your purpose on earth? What are you here for? What mission do you want to accomplish in your lifetime? Why do you do what you do in life?

In a nutshell—and with everything I've learned in my life so far—it's about bringing energy and passion to the table and creating a safe and inspiring space for solutions. This attitude helps others find what they really love (like the ideal job), what they can do best in life, and what makes them truly successful.

Part of my mission is also to support those around me with ideas and content. This can range from working on their (personal) strategy to helping others with sales, starting their own business, or living a healthier life—and more generally, to making work and life better for other people, which is then the basis for success for myself.

I want to support people on their personal development path to live the life they want to lead in harmony with their environment. Creating a safe and energetic space helps them to find the right solutions. Everyone who comes into my circle should win, gain, learn, or develop something useful.

Working with people in matchmaking (especially recruiting) and business development is a great fit for me. The core of my mission here on earth is to make others (people and companies) more successful in finding the most appropriate job, business partner or solution.

Question 5: Where are you going in your life from today? And with whom?

From today on, I will work even more internationally, ideally with people who share the same or similar values.

I will put more emphasis on making owners (especially private equity) and students more successful with my matchmaking, problem-solving, and business development skills. I will also look for products and services that enable good cooperation between humans and machines in my field (especially in matchmaking or business development), so that both can focus on what they do best.

Question 6: What is the joy—and what is the risk—of being or working with you?

The joy is that you will always get a lot of energy, ideas, and a solution-oriented positive spirit from me. I will help you to carry on or to find and take a different path. And you will learn, laugh, and receive important impulses for your own development and success. Part of the joy is that you can trust me completely.

The risk is that my plans are sometimes quite ambitious (maybe even too ambitious), which could potentially bring some turmoil and might even take some energy away. I am working on that. The joy of full trust has a downside too. The risk is that if you betray me once, you're out of my game.

Summary of your core, your uniqueness, your "certain something"

As a list of bullet points, here are the opportunities and possibilities that open up when you work with me:

- Creating new energy and generating profound solution ideas (even solutions you would never have dared to dream of).
- Being in a completely safe space.
- Being treated respectfully, personally, and in an honest and transparent way.

- Working with a generalist where collaboration is the name of the game.
- Finding a long-term buddy by your side.
- Learning in a very passionate and positive way.
- Exploring options for moving forward (going the experimental route).
- Getting full attention and a clear focus on delivering results for any team, job, or task.
- Achieving something new or different in your life (becoming more successful, happier, freer, more efficient, more satisfied).
- Getting the chance to improve by being challenged, to grow while enjoying life, to live respectfully in your environment, and to be inspired to develop yourself.
- Being successful together.

All of that comes with the following risks, however:

- The risk of overstretching.
- The risk of exceeding time limits.

The three sides of a coin (and how to find that "certain something" in a company)

If you ask a company owner (or top manager) these questions, they can help to reveal the essence of the company's uniqueness. Let me illustrate this once again with an example.

The example is Snigel (*snigel.com*), an award-winning international ad tech company. Snigel helps websites maximize their advertising revenue. It is one of three Irish companies to make the FT 1000—the *Financial Times*' list of Europe's fastest growing companies—for 2021. Snigel also ranked highly in Deloitte Ireland's *Fast 50* Index for both 2020 and 2021. I am related to one of the founders, and while writing this book I have also had the honor of advising and mentoring Snigel's management team. As a result, I have some deep insights into the company, so I can answer the questions almost as if it were my own.[1]

Actually, you can think of me as being hooked on Snigel's story. In fact, that is the main goal of a great story, to get your stakeholders so hooked that they can tell the company's story to others as if it were their own. To achieve this goal, a story must be real and authentic. It should contain both positive and negative elements, both light and shade, or it will not reflect reality. It always raises doubts for me (and I'm sure I'm not alone) when a company's story is filled only with positive elements, leaving out any risks, challenges, or fears. There are always two sides to a coin—a good one and a bad one (and sometimes even a third, if you flip a coin and set it in motion).

In terms of telling your story, this could mean that you should always strive to include both the good and the bad sides (the usual two sides of a coin) of your "certain something," and never stop looking for those parts that you cannot see at first glance. Remember that new characteristics and behaviors can emerge as you move and turn, whether you are a person or a company (this is like the third side of the coin, when you rotate it and it is in motion).

So let me try to answer our six questions for Snigel:

Question 1: What are Snigel's core values?

Snigel's core values are:

- Authenticity
- Care for family and friends
- Honesty and freedom
- Efficiency and speed
- High quality
- Creativity
- A mentality of empowering others
- Money orientation

- Profit sharing
- Agnosticism
- Caring
- Experimenting

Question 2: What is special/unique about Snigel that other people may or may not notice? What do other people say is special about Snigel?

At Snigel, you can work from anywhere (as long as you are performing well and the Wi-Fi is working). It started with the owners traveling around the world in a camper van. One of the founders is from Sweden, and they felt like a snail on tour (including the snail shell), so they named their new venture Snigel (Swedish for snail—so someone who travels around with their 'house'—a camper).

As the company grew, friends of the owners who brought valuable skills or unique qualities joined the team. Each team member was trusted completely (as friends are). At Snigel, there was always a clear focus on making clients happier and more successful, so the company could be seen as an "enabling boutique."

Products were created based on a deep understanding of the market and customer needs and were always tested with lead customers first. The "who" always took precedence over the "what."

Question 3: What have been the key events in Snigel's company history—those that have formed the company up to this moment? How do these key events influence the company's behavior (and maybe even its values)?

Snigel started out with a service for publishers. They came out with a digital product that worked really well. So did the remote model of organizing work. Two of the founders came from Google, which helped them start with a network of contacts that quickly turned into a solid customer base.

The founders had a big dream—to create a company that would be able to hire the best people in the world by offering a unique way to work remotely (this was long before Covid-19 made the remote work model popular). Remote work would save people time, since they wouldn't have to commute to an office, and it would energize them, since they could choose to live wherever they wanted. The concept also saved Snigel a lot of investment in office space.

This dream—and the passionate pursuit of that dream—also paved the way for testing new products and processes with customers and developing new markets, usually through an experimental approach. Long before design thinking became *en vogue*, Snigel worked with prototypes and minimum viable products—solutions that were "good enough" but not yet fully refined and finalized. But they came out at the right time. The "Sniglers" could be considered game-changers in the way they built their company and designed their products.

Question 4: What is Snigel's purpose on earth? What is Snigel's mission? Why does the Snigel team do what they do?

Snigel's mission is to make others more successful and prosperous by being a transparent, trustworthy partner for the long term (for customers, employees, partners, and owners).

Question 5: Where does Snigel go from here? And with whom?

After the founder-CEO and majority owner decided to step down for personal and business reasons (they did not see themselves as the perfect fit for the next stage of scaling), two managers (the former COO and the Director of Sales) stepped into a co-CEO role. The founder-CEO has sold his majority stake to a private equity firm, as they had more experience and resources to finance the next step in Snigel's growth story, which is strongly focused on scaling the existing business model to the next level, further internationalizing the business, and especially growing through mergers and acquisitions.

Question 6: What is the joy—and what are the risks—of working with Snigel?

One of the great joys of working at Snigel is the high degree of freedom. You also get to work with highly solution-oriented people in an environment where both the work and the results (profits) are shared.

The risk is that in a purely online company with 100% remote work, you might feel a little lonely from time to time. This can also sometimes lead to misunderstandings or, as Sniglers would call the downside of online communication, being "lost in space."

There is also a risk that the owner's ambitious scaling plans will overstretch the existing corporate system, and that the Snigel spirit of making a difference for customers will be subordinated to a (too) strong focus on money on the part of the new owners.

Summary of Snigel's core, uniqueness, or "certain something"

In summary, here are the opportunities and possibilities that open up when you work with Snigel:

- To be able to perform and be free in many ways.
- The chance to be the most authentic version of yourself.
- To be able to work in a very experimental and less formalized environment.
- To be self-organized.
- To become an enabler for the customer.
- To be successful through making others successful.
- To work in a very entrepreneurial scale-up environment.
- To work with colleagues who could become friends.

- To be part of a company that is changing "the rules of the game."
- To make a lot of money (without always being focused on it).

And here are the risks of working with Snigel:

- The risk of being overstretched.
- The risk of being lonely because you hardly see and meet your co-workers.
- The risk of being too money-oriented

The answers to these six questions and the resulting summary should provide a good basis for formulating your story for different stakeholder groups. They will help you define the what and why of your company. In a next step, it is important to clarify *how* and *where* you will tell your story—and especially *to whom* you will tell it.

This also brings us to the question of identifying the relevant stakeholders. This is related to the idea of concentric circles. If you look at Figure 2.1, you will see circles that are closer to the center. This is where you will find the partners and stakeholders with whom you have stronger ties and tend to communicate a lot. However, network theory suggests that we also need weak ties (which can be especially useful when you are trying to recruit someone or find a job).

So who do you tell your story to? Well, it may sound simple, but the key to success is to tell the story about your "certain something" to everyone you meet—whether they are near or far, whether you meet them in person or communicate with them online. When your team members and other stakeholders also start telling your story, you will get a multiplier effect that will help you get a lot more people excited about it. Take every opportunity to tell your story!

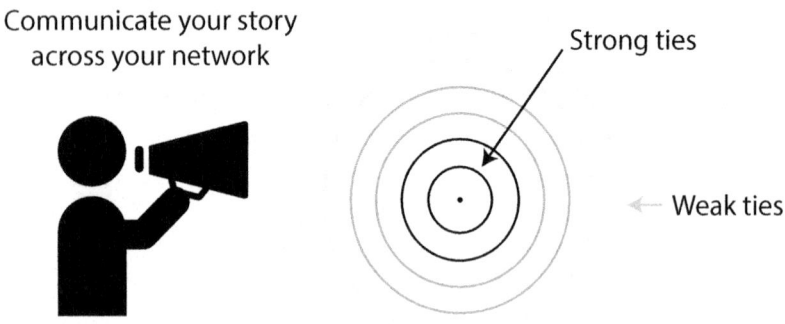

Figure 2.1 The concentric circles of your network

To continue our example, here is how Snigel's management might tell the company's story to key stakeholders:

- **To investors:** *"Do you want to work with great people who are authentic, solution-oriented and have relentless energy to create valuable products that make their clients more successful—and grow as their clients grow? You'll get that from the team at Snigel, the first ad tech company to go carbon neutral."* The message could be delivered at pitching events, investor matchmaking meetings (e.g., in a shared office space) or online conferences, or to advisors who match companies with investors, for example on LinkedIn or Twitter.
- **To customers:** *"If you want to be served in a way that helps you become more successful, if you want a trusted partner who is always there for you, who listens to you, and who helps you beyond ad tech when you need it—work with us. We will be your extended team."* The message could be delivered in the company's existing networks, on the company website, and to potential customers and partners at fairs, conferences, or online meetings. Every customer meeting can be used to get the message across.

- **To employees:** *"If you like living wherever you want (wherever Wi-Fi works), if you want to be independent while being prepared to deliver outstanding results, if you are an authentic person interested in long-term relationships, if you care about making a difference and being heard, if success really means something to you—join our team."* The message could be delivered on the company website, in every job ad, on job boards, at HR and recruiting events, in every interview or contact with a candidate, and to recruiting networks (which is one of the best ways to attract new employees).

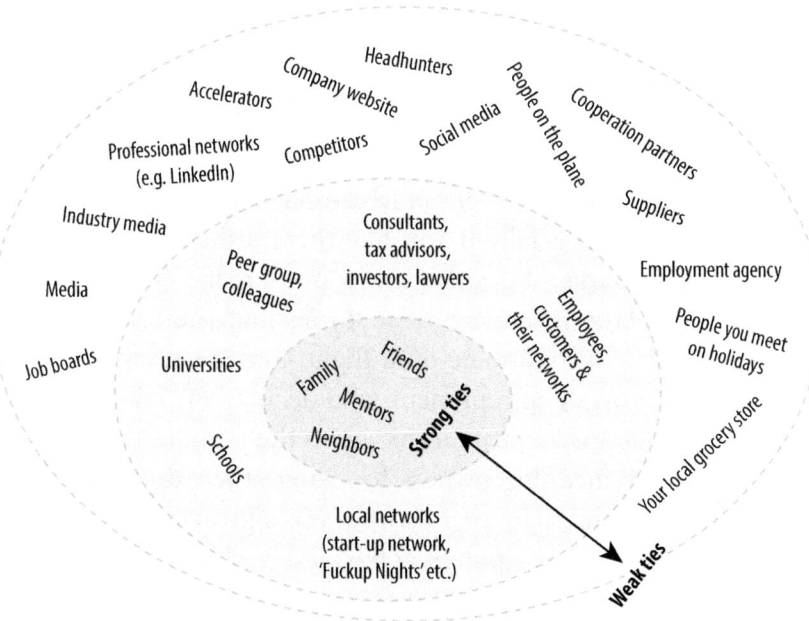

Figure 2.2 "Tell your network"

Figure 2.2 gives you more ideas about where and to whom you might tell your story. As you will notice, some channels are more time-consuming and costly than others. Most of the communication channels are self-explanatory, while some may seem a bit "strange" to you, at least at first sight. Let me quickly explain a few that might fall into the latter category:

- **The grocery store:** Everybody needs groceries. If you have a cool poster and they allow you to post it in a local grocery store, then go for it. Think about how you might be wandering along the windows, not looking for anything in particular, and then suddenly be drawn to something, like that great story poster from a great employer.
- **The employment agency:** Some people think that you cannot find great and enthusiastic people through an employment agency. I would still advocate giving it a try. Even if you only find one great employee, it is definitely worth telling your story.
- **Your neighbors:** Never underestimate the network of your neighbors (especially if you like them, otherwise it wouldn't work, of course—but that's true for other channels too).
- **On the plane:** There are great stories that you can hear from (and tell) your seatmate on a flight, like the story that I was once told by an entrepreneur who decided to create dog food made from insect protein (based on the premise that it is easier to convince dog owners to change their dog's diet to be carbon neutral than their own). It was a great pitch for me as a dog owner and as a potential business partner.

The picture of potential communication channels is far from being complete, but it might help you as a trigger for your further creative thinking. If you have other channels that work particularly well for you, please just let me know! (You are most welcome to contact me at *office@barbara-stampf.at*.)

In my experience, the best communication channel—and the best way to multiply your story—is your employees. They can be great ambassadors who can tell others about your "certain something" as a company in the most authentic way. You can learn more about turning your employees into superspreaders of your story in Chapter 3.

DEVELOP YOUR RECRUITING SKILLS

Recruitment tells a story

1. How do you answer the six questions in this chapter for yourself? How do you summarize the results? What is your own unique core, your personal "certain something"?
2. How do you answer the six questions for your venture or company? What is the core or the "certain something" of your business?

Recruitment is an "inside-out" job (or why employer branding should come last)

This chapter explores how to create an authentic story that resonates with stakeholders by taking an "inside-out" approach. It emphasizes developing your company's narrative based on your internal values and identity before focusing on employer branding. I will explain how to craft a powerful message that attracts potential employees and other stakeholders. At the same time, I will highlight the risks of focusing solely on stakeholder expectations with an "outside-in" approach, which can result in a story that is superficially appealing but lacks authenticity, potentially creating a disconnect between internal culture and external perceptions.

From "outside-in" to "inside-out"

In the previous chapter, we focused on discovering your company's "personal story" and what kind of character your company has. In this chapter, we will dig a little deeper and try to find out what elements you should include in your story to make it highly attractive to your stakeholders, and especially to potential candidates.

You might rightly ask if focusing on those elements should have been the starting point for developing our story in the first place. In my experience, there's a risk involved in such an approach. If you squint too much at these attractors, you run the risk of bowing too much to what people want to hear rather than what your company is really all about. This may lead to the production of glossy marketing materials, but the vibes will no longer be noticeable once you are inside the company, which means you are no longer authentic.

The trick is to do it the other way around: develop your inside story first, and then combine it with your stakeholders' expectations to differentiate yourself from the competition for talent (or products, investors, or collaborators).

This is an "inside-out" approach. It's a bit of a contrast to Dave Ulrich's "outside-in" view of HR management (see Figure 3.1).[1] Ulrich argued that the HR function must create value not only for employees and managers, but also for other stakeholders. In his view, HR—as well as other departments within an organization—must focus on creating value for external stakeholders such as customers, owners, and business partners by finding and developing great employees. HR also plays a role in providing employees with what they need to get customers to buy and come back for more. That's the real core of the HR work.

This could mean, for example, helping a sales manager or a developer grow the ability to understand customer needs. It's therefore an essential HR task to deeply understand the expectations of external stakeholders and match them with the expectations and capabilities of employees—and to close any gaps between the two sides. For example, if friendliness is a key criterion for your customers when they evaluate your service center, you need to hire or train the friendliest people and reward them for positive customer feedback on friendliness. It would also be great if you could help your customer service agents to regularly reflect on what specific expectations customers have regarding agent friendliness.

According to Dave Ulrich, the "outside-in" view should be a guiding star that helps HR professionals create value and impact for all key stakeholders.

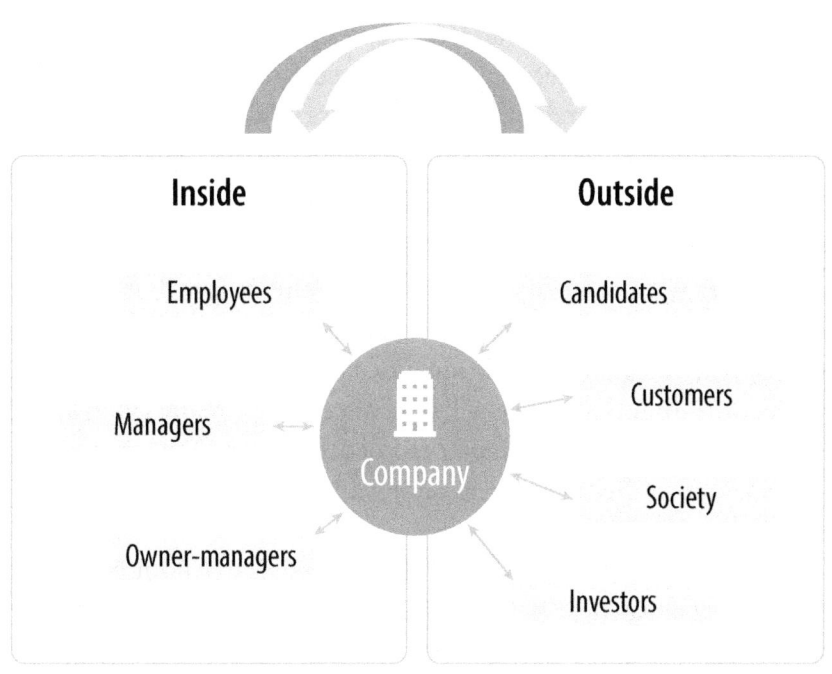

Figure 3.1 The "outside-in" and "inside-out" views of human resources management (building on the ideas of Dave Ulrich)

While I am a big fan of Dave Ulrich and his relentless drive to focus HR professionals on creating real impact, I believe that in recruitment, we need to take a more nuanced view. We can approach the challenge of attracting the best people from at least two different angles:

- **Angle 1:** In line with what we have just discussed, it makes a lot of sense to take an "outside-in" view first as a basis for preparing the list of job requirements that employees need to meet to be able to perform well in their jobs. (We will also take a closer look at how this works in Chapter 4.)

- **Angle 2:** To be able to attract people to your organization (from a very personal perspective), you need to start from the inside out. You must first clarify who you are, and then tell your story authentically so that potential candidates are drawn to it.

If you start from the outside, you run the risk of writing a story that does not really reflect who you are, but only what you think candidates want to hear (I know I've said this before, but it's really essential). If your employer marketing message doesn't match your true spirit, you may be painting a desired image—an "outside-in" projection—but that image will fade once people really get to know you. The further away the image is from reality, the less trustworthy you will appear because you are not walking the talk (i.e., what you say is not what you do).

At least after some time, this will feel awkward. And it can make people feel cheated or betrayed from the first day they start working for you. Obviously, this is not a good basis for creating a great employer brand.

You can be sure that the negative feelings you create when you choose to follow this "outside-in" projection path will be communicated to other candidates, too. Eventually, you will run the risk of people laughing at you. You may even get those online reviews you never wanted to see about your company. And you may become one of those companies that I get a message from like: "Hey, Barbara, yes, they say that, but in reality, our boss behaves very differently—and that's exactly our problem." Not the best outlook, right?

The six key elements that stakeholders are looking for in your story

Now let's look at the common elements that customers, partners, owners, and employees look for in a company's story. I will then explain how you can link your story (see Chapter 2) to these elements and how you can create a message that is truly unique to you and sets you apart from your competitors.

I have worked with many companies in various roles—as an employee, consultant, recruiter, trainer, and partner—and have observed a few common expectations among stakeholders. Of course, every company is generally expected to be sustainably profitable, and to deliver the key outcomes for its stakeholders—high quality products and services for customers, decent salaries for employees, and bills paid on time for suppliers. But there are also some more implicit, or "tacit," expectations, which I will try to summarize in the six elements of a compelling company story.

Element #1: Ethos (integrity, honesty, trustworthiness)[2]

The GLOBE study was a massive research project that looked at preferred leadership qualities in 62 countries around the world.[3] It revealed that there was one quality that all employees were looking for in their leaders, no matter which country they came from. That quality was integrity (honesty, trustworthiness). We all, whether we are in the role of an employee or a customer, look for people we can rely on, someone who walks the talk. This doesn't mean that a leader can't change course, but when they do so, they will also tell you why it's necessary (with good arguments—see Element #3).

This is a leadership quality that is becoming increasingly important in a world that has just been shaken by a pandemic and is generally characterized by rapid change, and in an environment where companies are being scrutinized for their environmental footprint and overall ESG (environmental, social, and governance) performance. I am talking about the real ESG performance here, not the "nicely packaged" (or greenwashed) version. (The younger generation is becoming increasingly allergic to that.)

Thus, this ethos creates or requires attitudes and behaviors in top executives, managers, and employees such as

- Being true to yourself, your motives, and your values
- Telling the truth to your partners
- Being honest about how you feel about others or a situation
- Acknowledging your mistakes
- Having good intentions to lead people to a "better place"
- Being tough on substance and results, but soft on people ("*Fortiter in re, suaviter in modo*"—gentle in manner, firm in action—as the ancient Romans would have put it)
- Being interested in other people's opinions, ideas, and impact
- Accepting that facts are friendly and asking for action, not packaging

Ethos (which means character in ancient Greek) is also the backbone of what is currently discussed under the term "psychological safety," which is widely recognized as a key building block of successful teams.[4] Just think about what it takes for you to feel safe. When can you rely on a leader or your colleagues to walk the talk and really mean what they say by actively doing it themselves? This will always be a foundation for the other elements we will discuss.

Element #2: Pathos (inspiration)[2]

People are drawn to positive vibes and energizing environments. So, when do you experience these? Usually when leaders or colleagues inspire you, when they create a space in which you can learn, grow, and develop a deeper passion for your work. Such positive energy can fuel both your creativity and your productivity.

Positive energy is the cornerstone of a happy and healthy life. One of my mentors once described a good leader as literally raising the temperature and energy in the room so that people can more easily find better solutions to their own challenges. The idea is not to tell people what to do, but to create a place of vibrant energy where they can find solutions for themselves.

Having pathos is a key characteristic of an inspirational leader. It creates or requires attitudes and behaviors in top leaders, managers, and employees such as

- Recognizing positive things and communicating in a positive and constructive way
- Showing respect and appreciation, respecting the whole personality of other people with all their bright and dark sides (i.e., the whole uniqueness of a person)
- Complimenting people on success and on making progress
- Using positive humor
- Giving gifts (tangible or intangible) to thank and appreciate people
- Asking curious questions and being deeply interested in hearing the answers
- Being happy and honest people themselves, accepting their own strengths and limitations, and seeing themselves in a positive light
- Being optimistic about both the bright and the dark sides of life
- Communicating from and to the heart

Element #3: Logos (having a clear "why")

People want to understand why decisions are made, why things are done, how they are done, why a certain goal is set and why it is chosen over another, why one person is hired (and another is not), why someone is promoted (or not), or why product A (and not product B) is developed.

So you need to justify your "why" for everything that happens in the workplace (e.g., for processes, products, structures, emotions, results, and impacts). *Logos* refers to the quality of being "logical," of being able to explain why something is best done in a certain way. This creates or requires attitudes and behaviors from top leaders, managers, and employees such as:

- Developing clear and understandable reasons for their decisions (and being able to communicate them clearly)
- Finding reasonable conclusions (or even new ideas) based on data
- Forwarding valid and logical arguments
- Being curious to understand the context (e.g., laws, policies, or other important contextual factors) to develop good reasons for their decisions
- Being clear and concise in their reasoning

Element #4: Autonomy[5]

Most people like to be free—to show and live their individuality and uniqueness. The word "autonomy" comes from the Greek word *autónomos*, where *auto* means "self" and *nomos* means "rule" or "law," so we are literally talking about "making your own rules or laws."

Having autonomy seems easier in some jobs and companies than in others. A factory worker producing a household appliance on shift work will obviously have less freedom than a marketing manager responsible for designing the next marketing campaign for their company. (But even factory workers have some freedom, for example in how they communicate with their co-workers.)

So while the degree of autonomy (and perceived autonomy) varies from function to function, most people like to be "free" to decide how to work. A certain degree of autonomy gives them the feeling of being independent, being able to pursue their own goals and align them with their values, and taking their own decisions. Becoming autonomous is one of the most important processes we go through in the transition from adolescence to adulthood, and of course we all strive to maintain this state throughout our adult lives (although we usually also want to keep our inner child alive as a source of inspiration).

This is one reason why flextime arrangements have been so appealing to many employees. It is a way to make people happy and satisfied with their work and their lives, to give them—within certain limits—the autonomy to decide when they want to work. In my view, flextime has become something of a minimum requirement for providing the autonomy to balance work and individual needs.

What I have also experienced and observed is that there is often a gap between perceived autonomy and real autonomy. Most of the time, people in many functions have more autonomy than they actually realize, but their fears keep them from trying things out and enjoying the fruits of their attempts. Promoting autonomy in an organization requires attitudes and behaviors such as:

- Trusting other people to do their best
- Seeing people as "entrepreneurs of their lives"
- Having the courage to try different ways of giving autonomy to different functions
- Being creative in finding the right way to promote autonomy

- Viewing leadership as an opportunity to define appropriate boundaries within which people can freely make decisions and act
- Believing that it is almost always possible to identify win-win situations for employees and leaders, and that we just need to look for them
- Experiencing the different dimensions of autonomy (regarding time, location, or thoughts)

Element #5: Purpose (or impact)

I believe that everyone wants to live a life in which they can make a difference in their relationships with others. It is just in our nature as human beings that we want to make a real impact on the world and thus lead a meaningful life. (There may be a minority of the world's population who also like to destroy value, but they're probably not the ones you want to work with.)

Just as personal preferences for autonomy vary (some people need more, some a little less), there are also very different perspectives about purpose. What one person finds meaningful may not resonate with another.

When I ask students what purpose they want to work for, they very often answer that they want to help others to be more successful, to become stronger, and to get products and services that will make their lives easier. So, it is mainly about empowering others, enabling them to achieve their own goals and live a better life.

Helping and supporting others seems to be very fulfilling. In fact, this is consistent with studies showing that when people meditate on compassion, their brain produces gamma waves that can make them happier.[6] If just thinking about helping others can make you happy, having a job where you can actually do something good for others can have an even greater positive impact on your life.

The good news is that there is a huge amount of purposeful work out there, in existing businesses, in new ventures, and in countless ideas that could still be turned into businesses. And an increasing number of investors are including purpose as a key factor in their investment decisions, too.

Purpose as a key element of your company's story requires attitudes and behaviors such as:

- A continuous quest for what really matters
- Putting value creation for multiple stakeholder groups at the center of your business
- Seeing and believing that people really want to make a difference
- Trying to find out (through careful observation and listening) what people really care about
- Accepting that people have different purposes (and that making money is only one of them, but can be very important to some people)
- Helping people find out what they really have energy for

Element #6: Mastery (or learning)

There is another thing that everyone loves—the idea of getting better and better at what you do. Why else would you spend hours practicing your guitar, playing volleyball, or knitting? It is that feeling of satisfaction you get when you get to the next level, whether it is baking that incredible cake, playing online games, or doing your job. It gives us a lot of motivation to learn something new, to grow, and to increase our ability to create something valuable for ourselves or others.

Enabling mastery requires attitudes and behaviors such as:

1. Practice (learning by doing)
2. Being curious and eager to learn

3. Being attentive to your surroundings and taking every opportunity to learn
4. Being a good observer and listener (again, with the clear goal of learning something new)
5. Being ambitious and never giving up
6. Always striving to make progress

In summary, what employees and other stakeholders typically expect from a company is this: **ethos** (integrity and trustworthiness), **pathos** (inspiration) and **logos** (a clear "why"), combined with a requisite degree of **autonomy**, a worthwhile **purpose** and an inspiring learning environment in which they can make progress in their **mastery** of skills that enable them to create something that matters to them and to others. When they find such an environment, employees will make an impact almost naturally,[7] as long as they are not blocked by negative emotions.

Making an impact with your story

So, how can you use your company's "personal story" and the "inside-out" approach to attract talented people and other relevant stakeholders to your organization? And how can you ensure that your story focuses on the key elements that people seem to be hungry for?

Here is how to do it step-by-step (see Figure 3.2):

1. Start with the key points of your story that you have identified in Chapter 2 (represented by A to E in Figure 3.2).
2. Juxtapose them with the expectations of candidates or other key stakeholders in terms of offering ethos, pathos, logos, autonomy, purpose, and mastery (represented by 1 to 5 in Figure 3.2).
3. Check where the key points of your story match the expectations (see the 'Combined' column in Figure 3.2).

4. Focus on those elements of the story that are unique to your organization from the perspective of the relevant stakeholders, i.e. real differentiators from the competition (in this example A 1, 5 and E 1 are unique, while C 3 is not unique to your company).

Based on the 6 elements of a great company story
↓

Story	Expectations	Combined	Unique
A	1	A 1, 5	A 1, 5
B	2	B	
C	3	C 3	
D	4	D	
E	5	E 1	E 1

Figure 3.2 Uncovering the authentic "core" of your story with the "inside-out" approach[8]

Following on from the example in Chapter 2, let's look again at the ad tech company Snigel. We have identified as the "core" of Snigel's story (see p. 40) the following opportunities and possibilities that open up when working with Snigel:

- *To be able to perform and be free* → linked to AUTONOMY
- *To have the chance to be the most authentic version of yourself* → linked to ETHOS
- *To be able to work in a very experimental and less formalized environment* → linked to AUTONOMY

- *To be self-organized* → linked to AUTONOMY
- *To become an enabler for the customer* → linked to PURPOSE
- *To be successful through making others successful* → linked to PURPOSE
- *To work in a very entrepreneurial scale-up environment* → linked to MASTERY
- *To work with colleagues who could become friends* → linked to PURPOSE
- *To be part of a company that is changing the rules of the game* → linked to MASTERY and AUTONOMY
- *To make a lot of money (without always being focused on it)* → linked to PURPOSE, ETHOS and PATHOS

Now let's match that up with what's relevant to the target audience of potential employees:

- Working from anywhere at any time (being autonomous)—maybe also deciding what to work on
- Being entrepreneurial and independent
- Participating in the financial success of the company
- Being able to act in a very authentic way (being true to oneself)
- Working with and learning from people in an international environment
- Enabling customer progress through technology
- Learning from mistakes

In Table 3.1, you can see which of these requirements of the potential employees are a good fit with the points of the story we identified earlier as highly relevant to stakeholders.

The final step is to check which of the relevant points in your story are truly unique in a way that differentiates you from your direct competitors.

Points in the "inside-out" story that are relevant to stakeholders	Linked to	Fits requirements of potential employees/future applicants
To be able to perform and be free	AUTONOMY	Working from anywhere at any time (being autonomous)—maybe also deciding what to work on
To have the chance to be the most authentic version of yourself	ETHOS	Being able to act in a very authentic way (being true to oneself)
To be self-organized	AUTONOMY	Working from anywhere at any time (being autonomous)—maybe also deciding what to work on
To become an enabler for the customer	PURPOSE	Enabling customer success through technology
To be successful through making others successful	PURPOSE	Enabling customer success through technology
To work in a very entrepreneurial scale-up environment	MASTERY	Learning from mistakes

Table 3.1 Matching relevant points in a company story with the requirements of a particular stakeholder group (in this case, potential employees)

In the case of Snigel, these unique factors are:

- Enabling customer success through technology.
- The ability to work remotely from anywhere at any time—perhaps even the ability to choose to work on what you really think is important (autonomy in many directions).
- An open communication climate that encourages authenticity, values honesty, welcomes constructive feedback, and embraces suggestions for improvement.

- A creative, entrepreneurial, and solution-oriented environment (with lots of opportunities for enhancing mastery and learning).

Using an "inside-out" approach, we have now uncovered the authentic "core" of what is sometimes called an *employer brand*—the ideal way to position yourself to potential employees.

While I have outlined a structured method for developing your compelling story with an "inside-out" approach, you can also tackle this challenge more intuitively. One way is to use images that represent your leadership team's core values and beliefs. For example, you might imagine your leadership team as a group climbing a mountain together, symbolizing teamwork and growth, or as people celebrating success, showing a positive and supportive environment. Or you could use animal metaphors to represent your leaders.

You could then apply the same method for the candidates (or other stakeholders) you want to attract. For instance, how could candidates who might feel unsure about a climb still feel safe with your team? Or how would those who prefer quieter settings feel about joining your culture? When comparing your path with competitors who offer similar journeys, where would candidates feel more at home? What will it be like for employees to work for a team of leaders who see themselves as dolphins? In this way, you can create both a compelling story and a visual representation of it.

Whichever approach you choose, a well-crafted and well-communicated "inside-out" story will ensure that your company's true essence shines through, attracting the right talent and fostering trust and long-term alignment between your company's goals and those of the candidates.

DEVELOP YOUR RECRUITING SKILLS

Reflecting on recruitment as an "inside-out" job

1. Try to get honest and open feedback from your stakeholders about how they see you.
2. Listen to yourself: What does the feedback that you are receiving about your company trigger in you? Discuss your feelings with a friend or trusted colleague.
3. What do you want to keep and what do you want to change about yourself and your business to ignite your own positive energy and make you even more passionate about what you do?
4. What image would best reflect you, your company, and your leadership style?

The process of recruiting the best team

This chapter provides a step-by-step approach to recruiting. At each step, we will focus on the benefits to both the candidate and the hiring organization. After all, that's what any well-designed process should be about: delivering effective (and easily replicable) benefits to users. Such a process can then also form the basis for digitization, after clarifying which parts of the process are better performed by humans or by a machine in order to serve the parties effectively.

I thought long and hard about whether I should write a chapter on the recruitment process, especially since you can find a lot about it in HR textbooks. (And you'll probably remember that at the beginning of this book, I expressed concern that we tend to place too much emphasis on the process when it comes to hiring people.)

But then something came to mind that fits with my way of thinking about how processes can help you succeed in recruiting—the idea of looking at the "classic" steps of recruiting from two different perspectives: your own needs/expectations/benefits as a recruiter, manager, or entrepreneur on the one hand, and the needs of the candidate on the other. In this way, we will explore how the process can benefit all parties involved, so that it becomes the servant rather than the master. This is how I would like to see processes and process steps in business in general—always with a clear view of how they can serve people.

So let's take a look at the 12 key steps of a professional recruiting process (see Figure 4.1)—and how they can benefit everyone involved.

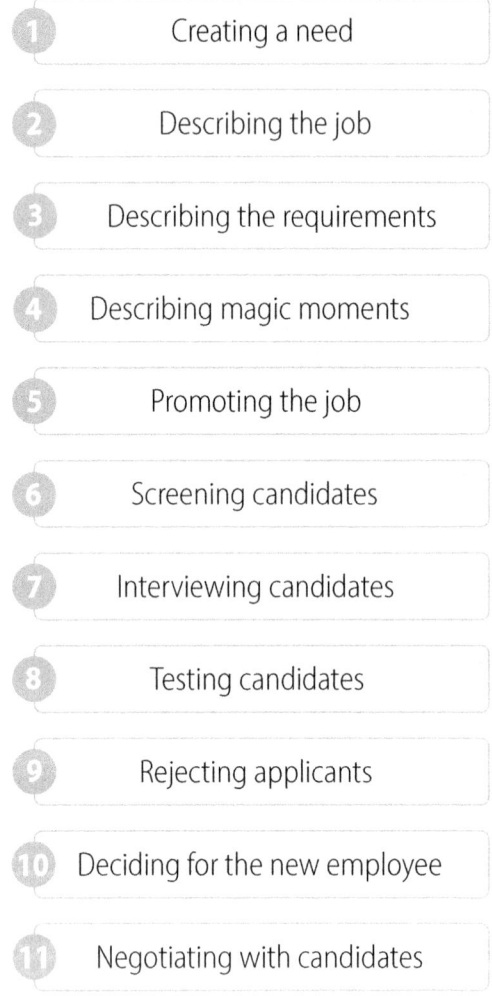

Figure 4.1 The 12 key steps of a professional recruiting process

Step 1: Creating a need

You may hire a new person to replace someone who has left the company, you may have a vacancy because you are expanding your business, or you may simply want to meet potential candidates to build a talent pool without having a specific job in mind. Whatever your need, both you and the candidate should know exactly why you are approaching the market.

Why is this relevant to you and the candidate?

By understanding the recruitment need, the candidate will learn more about the company's situation (replacement, growth opportunities, etc.) and the company's culture (why is the replacement necessary, did the former employee decide to leave the employer or are there other reasons). In general, it would be very helpful for a candidate to know the percentage of voluntary departures from the company (which we also call the "turnover rate") and to understand the reasons. This could provide important information about a company's culture.

It can also be beneficial for both parties if the candidate can estimate how long it will take the company to make a final decision. When hiring high potentials to build a talent pool, a long-term perspective is usually applied in recruitment, and it could also take much longer to make the final hiring decision.

Step 2: Describing the job

To describe a job well, you must first be clear about its goals and outcomes, as well as the day-to-day tasks associated with it. You must ask yourself what tasks must be performed in order to be successful in the job and achieve or exceed the expected results (e.g., holding meetings with key customers or analyzing the market to increase profits).

A goal is what you want to accomplish in a certain amount of time. Ideally, it should be defined in a "SMART" way. SMART typically stands for specific, measurable, achievable, relevant, and timed. It basically means that the goal should be as specific as possible so that you can measure whether or not it has been achieved. The "A" in SMART could also be interpreted as *attractive* to both the job holder and the company, or as *ambitious*.

There are two philosophies for dealing with the "A" because *achievable* can contradict *ambitious* and *attractive*. Setting ambitious stretch goals means making them less achievable. With this approach, you are shooting for the moon (and the worst that can happen is that you end up somewhere else in the universe). Alternatively, you could try to strike a balance between attractive and realistic elements. Or maybe you just define the goals in a very realistic (and therefore achievable) way because that better suits your culture.

Once you have identified its main goals and tasks, you can add more information about the job and its framework conditions. What is the size and structure of the team? Who reports to whom? What are the work hours? How much travel is involved? Are there any special responsibilities associated with the position? What is the remuneration for the position?

Try to include all the elements necessary to describe the job to someone outside your immediate circle. A good job description should pass the "grandma test." This means that your grandmother will understand the key duties and responsibilities without being an industry insider and without being familiar with the company jargon or the latest trends in the field. If absolutely necessary, the technical side of a job can be excluded from the "grandma test," but it can also be useful to describe the value of performing a technical task in a way that people without a specialist background can understand.

Why is this relevant to you and the candidate?

Creating a job description helps you as a hiring manager think through the key elements of a job before explaining it to someone else. In my opinion, this tool is often underestimated. Some even consider it unnecessary, perhaps because the forms that need to be filled out (provided by HR or administration) are often cluttered and confusing. Job descriptions are also often copied and pasted from other job descriptions. This is something I've never understood—how can you get other people excited about a job that you haven't thought through well, and that you haven't taken the time and effort to describe in an attractive way?

It is important for candidates to understand what is expected of them. What are the expected results of a particular position in a particular company? And this applies to every position, whether you are recruiting for the CEO, a business angel, a quality manager, or a new salesperson. It is an opportunity for candidates to understand if and how they believe they can achieve the required results. It is also a chance for candidates to get a better picture of the day-to-day tasks they would be expected to perform. It is also a chance for candidates to get their first glimpse of how the company designs a system of goals and how it structures work, which gives insight into the culture. A good job description is therefore an opportunity to look beyond the "what" of a job to the "why" and "how" of a job.

Steps 3 and 4: Describing the requirements and "magic moments"

The next two steps belong together—a bit like yin and yang. In the past, it used to be standard practice to derive all the skills necessary for successful job performance from the job description. However, as the competition for talent in the job market becomes increasingly fierce, I recommend that you not only focus on the company's needs, but also put yourself in the candidate's shoes. This means that you should be able to describe the candidate's requirements for a job and understand what "magic moments" they might experience on the job. "Magic moments" is a term coined by German HR management professor Armin Trost to describe strong positive emotions you can have when you are in a state of flow or experiencing success in a particular activity.[1] These are factors that can make a job highly attractive to top talent.

But let us start with the requirements of the company. There are several categories of requirements to consider:

- **Technical and methodological skills**, from a programming language that a programmer should know, to a specific business tool that an expert-level manager should be able to use, or business acumen that a member of a founding team should have.
- **Personal skills**, which describe specific behaviors based on certain values that a candidate must possess to be successful in a particular job, such as enthusiasm, punctuality, and high standards of work.
- **Social skills**, which describe certain behaviors displayed when working with different stakeholders, such as employees, customers, owners, and suppliers. This could include, for example, an open, outgoing, extroverted communication style, or the ability to resolve conflicts and find win-win solutions, or the ability to build balanced teams.

It is really important to describe these requirements in detail and then rank or prioritize them. Then it will be much easier for you to understand exactly what you are looking for in candidates, and it will be easier for candidates to understand exactly what the company needs.

These clearly defined job requirements then form the basis for evaluating résumés and assessing candidates' answers in interviews. In fact, it's hard to imagine effective interviews or assessments without them. If you don't know what you're looking for, how can you ask helpful questions in an interview or create an effective gamified online assessment tool?

Candidates also often criticize the superficiality of job advertisements and the fact that they contain a lot of "blah blah," headlines that can mean anything or nothing and that can be found in every company for every job. For example, "being communicative" is presented as an important qualification for a candidate. Have you ever seen an ad for someone who is taciturn or unable to work effectively in a team? What does "being communicative" really mean for your company? Are you looking for people who actively listen to their colleagues at work, who are able to speak up when they need support or face challenges? Or are you looking for people who are able to solve problems on their own and then only communicate the results or reach out to others when they hit a roadblock? There are a number of different interpretations of what it means to be "communicative" and you'd better be clear about what you really expect!

It's not uncommon that when I talk to two different clients, I get more than two different interpretations of what good communicative behavior means. This is not a mathematical phenomenon, but a social one. One of my clients, for example, after discussing the matter with me, came to the conclusion that what they really need are more independent and quiet producers of results, not extroverts who like to present themselves to others. Don't get me wrong — this is not about "black and white" or "0–1" requirements, it's about understanding the different shades of personal behavior that can make people successful in a given environment.

Think about examples of different behaviors that make people valuable contributors to your organization. This will help you make your requirements as specific as possible.

And don't forget to prioritize your requirements! Candidates will scoff at a job posting with "jack-of-all-trades" requirements. They know that such expectations are unrealistic, and that these ads neither reflect the reality of the company nor acknowledge the challenging conditions of the job market. Most importantly, those who place such ads fail to understand human nature—no one can excel at everything. Be realistic about your expectations instead of laying the groundwork for amusement and/or frustration.

Once you've adequately defined the job requirements, it's time to dive into the "magic moments" and look at the job through the employee's eyes. What aspects of their work do people or employees genuinely cherish? What energy and vibes does their work emanate? What positive emotions (such as joy, confidence, pride, appreciation, enthusiasm, fun, satisfaction, peacefulness, gratitude, serenity, and flow) are triggered by success in a particular role? What is the intrinsic appeal of the job? This is not about monetary rewards, which are extrinsic factors. "Intrinsic attraction" refers to the inherent qualities and fulfilling aspects of a job that go beyond external rewards and include elements such as meaningful engagement, personal satisfaction, and a sense of purpose.

"Magic moments" can come in many forms. For salespeople, for example, they can be found in their personal interactions with customers—the conversations they have with them on a business trip, the heart and soul they put into winning them over, the personal spirit they bring to the table, and the emotion they invest before a deal is signed. For sports coaches, it might be the deep joy of seeing children's eyes light up because they have learned something new that makes them very proud. For programmers, it might be a "magic moment" when the new software suddenly does what it is supposed to do, when the inner window to your deep joy suddenly opens because you have solved something important or achieved a goal you have been pursuing for a long time.

For others, it might even be a sense of security or stability in performing a repetitive task over and over again. I know this might sound a little strange to you. Can this really feel good? If it doesn't sound magical to you, it won't produce a positive emotional outcome for you. But that doesn't mean it can't be "magic" for others. We are all different, which is great, and it means that we are satisfied or positively emotionally touched by different aspects of work.

Why is this relevant to you and the candidate?

Clear job requirements are crucial for a cohesive recruitment process. Knowing precisely what you are looking for helps you assess whether candidates align with your needs. It will help you identify suitable people, focus on assessing the relevant aspects, and ask the right questions in the selection process. Describing the "magic moments" will help you highlight the positive aspects and emotions you can offer to candidates. Avoiding a "jack-of-all-trades" approach prevents candidates from struggling to fit your profile and keeps your organization focused on essential skills. You will not run the risk of being perceived as a company that exaggerates and is unable to focus on the skills that really matter.

It is much better to be authentic in describing what the job really entails. If you have the courage, you can even describe the negative emotions that can occur when things go wrong in the job. I recently saw an insurance company admit their high turnover and its causes, and describe how they would do things differently. This is a very open approach which means people know what to expect. Any job can evoke both positive and negative emotions, and including both provides a holistic view that attracts suitable candidates and effectively discourages unsuitable ones.

Do not underestimate emotions and feelings in the workplace! Candidates and employees may forget what you said and did, but they will never forget how you made them feel during the application process or in a particular job.[2]

Step 5: Promoting the job

If you have done your work in steps 1 through 4, promoting the job will be easy. Simply summarize the following information in either a written dossier or a short video for active candidates or in a story line for an outreach to passive candidates:[3]

- The reason for opening the position
- The main results/outcomes to be achieved in the role
- The main tasks to be performed
- The (crystal-clear) requirements of the job
- The "magic moments" the job offers

Ideally, you can then also complement the written or video ad with

- Your company's story (see Chapters 2 and 3)
- The benefits you offer
- The in-house development you offer
- The reporting line or team structure

A great advertisement will attract the right people while discouraging the wrong people from applying. It can play with words, colors, and images, or it can use humor to stand out from the crowd. The ideal ad will also make people who already work for you or are otherwise associated with you proud of the company. If you get feedback from someone who works with you that they saw the ad, appreciated it, and think it accurately represents your company, you are on the right track. When I worked at a semiconductor company, we took a picture of all 100 employees and had it signed by the CEO, thanking each of them for doing their best and achieving their goals. The employees loved it, and so did the applicants for jobs at the company. It was a topic of conversation for a long time.

Of course, the way you post the job will also depend on the advertising channels you use (see also Chapter 2). For example, you might use your company website, job boards (such as monster.com or Indeed, or other job search sites), LinkedIn, or other professional media. You might plan to use Google or social media ads. Or you may plan to actively seek passive candidates. Each medium has its limitations. For example, if you plan to target candidates on LinkedIn, you may want to use a shorter version of your job description and company story and focus on the key messages you want to convey.

If you want to contact a potential candidate directly, make a very personal approach by addressing them by name, telling them why you are contacting them and why you think they are an attractive candidate for the job (e.g., because of their experience in a particular industry or job role, or because of the people they are connected to). You might also include a brief description of your company and the open position. The right length depends on the candidate's preferences, but a good rule of thumb, if the message is personal, is to keep it concise and to the point.

I also always like to add a question or a cliffhanger (a teaser that makes the candidate curious) to engage the candidate in a discussion and get them to give feedback.

In my experience, the more personal your approach and the more confident you are that the job truly offers value for the candidate, the more likely they are to respond. Remember what we discussed in Chapter 1: Success comes from being the one who gives more than you take.

As an avid recruiter, I also see every outreach as a chance to connect with great people or build a talent pool, even if the job at hand might not be very attractive to them at the time. Of course, what I've told you is just my own outreach experience. You do not have to believe me. The most scientific (and usually successful) way is to run your own A/B tests to find out which outreach method produces the best results for you.

Why is this relevant to you and the candidate?

The job posting is your way, whether personally or as a company, of getting the word out that you have a job opening. If you have done your work in the previous steps of the recruiting process, all you need to do is package the information in a way that appeals to your target audience. You can also personally spread the word to your network, increasing your chances of finding a suitable candidate, or better yet, *the* most suitable candidate. A recruiting process that results in the one great candidate who then becomes an employee is the most effective one.

The benefit to the candidate—whether they are an active candidate or a passive candidate approached directly by you—is that they receive authentic and clear information about what they can expect from working at your company. They can also learn a lot about how the company operates from the way the ad is created and displayed. Every step a company takes during the application process reveals information to the candidate. And it's the same in reverse. Every step counts. If an ad is overselling, it says something. If an ad is overloaded, it says something. And when an ad stands out from the crowd because it is completely different, that says something, too.

Step 6: Screening candidates

Once your message has been delivered to the relevant audiences, the next step is to review the applications received from interested candidates. If you've reached out to potential candidates who may not proactively apply but who you've identified as a potential match, it's important to conduct this screening first. In this step, you evaluate candidates on professional or social media platforms and carefully consider how well their online profiles match the job requirements.

This is a highly analytical part of the recruiting process. You are analyzing factual information about candidates found in their résumés or on LinkedIn, ultimately leading to a decision about how well they fit the role. Some might argue that this is a job for machines, given their ability to compare and contrast vast amounts of data. While this is true to some extent, humans also process emotional data that machines struggle to identify or use effectively. When you read a résumé, you are not just processing the facts. Some things you read may also feel right or feel strange. We are currently looking for the best way for machines and humans to work together in this process. One undeniable advantage of machines seems to be their ability to potentially reduce bias, especially when emotions and generalizations are removed from the equation.[4]

So how do you analyze the facts? Do you just check the boxes: Is it the right industry? Does the candidate have the right amount of experience in the area you want? Are they from the right company? Do they have the right tenure with previous employers—or have they changed jobs a little too frequently?

You may be able to read between the lines of a profile, résumé, or cover letter. Many of my clients ask me if and how they can do this. It is indeed a challenging task! And I can only give you my personal view—based on many years of experience—of how I try to get a "smell" of the person behind the résumé. I always try to ask questions like:

- What is your first impression of what the candidate might need? (Write it down.)
- Have they worked in a corporate environment for a long time? What would it mean for them to move from a larger company to a smaller company? Or vice versa.
- Do they follow leaders, groups, or associations that are valued in your company on professional social media?
- Could they be looking for something you think you have to offer? Is there anything like an "open wish" that you could read in their profiles?

- What are your initial feelings about the candidate's fit?
- How does their summary statement or letter of motivation fit with what you are looking for? Does the whole letter seem more rational or more emotional?
- Are the candidate's profile and motivation letter spot on? Personal? With or without errors? Do these documents seem dedicated or passionate?
- Is there anything noticeable, awkward, or remarkable that leaves you with a question mark?
- Are there any gaps in the profile or résumé?

Write down your initial impressions, but then—and this is really important—give yourself an incubation period, some time to process the information you have gathered. It's a bit like good dough that needs time to rise to the right size; feelings need time to settle and generate useful insights.

Those initial feelings and reactions may help you check off key criteria for assessing a candidate's suitability, or they might even lead you to develop new criteria you hadn't considered before. Crafting the ideal job profile can, in this sense, be viewed as an iterative process, where your evaluation of the first candidates provides feedback for refining the profile. This approach is similar to design thinking, where you quickly release a prototype and then improve it over multiple cycles based on user feedback.

Keep in mind, however, that even with the most meticulous efforts to create an ideal job profile and thorough evaluation in selecting candidates, mistakes are inevitable in the hiring process. After all, recruiting involves human judgment, and the inherent nature of humans is such that certain facts, behaviors, and emotions may be overlooked.

With people involved on all fronts—candidates, employers, and even recruitment agencies like my own—mistakes can happen. The important thing is to quickly recognize when a mistake has been made and to take immediate corrective action. This correction can take many forms, such as adjusting the new hire's role, redefining the job, changing the supervisor, or even considering a move to another company. While such corrective action is essential, it is never easy because it requires an admission of error—a step that requires a certain amount of self-reflection. However, if you are unable to admit a mistake in your role as a manager or recruiter, you will create a very damaging situation for both the company and the candidate. Therefore, it is essential to have the courage to confront and correct any missteps.

What you need to be aware of is that your mind, and especially your emotions, naturally generate biases (our minds are simply bias-generating machines). This can include preferences based on appearance, regional origin, or educational background, or unfair dismissal of candidates who have taken unconventional paths, such as a sabbatical. The only thing we can do is be aware of this fact and ask ourselves regularly if we have fallen into a bias trap (you can also ask someone else to remind you to do this). If you think you're the only one who doesn't have prejudices and biases, you should consider whether you haven't just fallen into the trap yourself.

Candidates will also apply a screening process at their end. When writing a résumé or cover letter for a job, it is very important to research the company and develop questions that will be useful during the interview. They will ask themselves: What kind of company is this? What industry and markets do they operate in? What is their reputation in the labor market? What challenges do they face? What current information is available about them (e.g., in press releases)?

But there are also deeper questions for a candidate to consider:

- Why am I really applying for a job?
- What do I like (and dislike) about the job description?
- What is my first feeling about the job and the company when I read the job description?

- Where do I fit? Where do I not fit?
- Is there anything unique about me that would make me a perfect fit for the job?
- Why would I choose myself for the job (or not)?
- Who in my network might know more about this job/role, company, or boss?
- What are my hopes and concerns about this job offer?

So when you create your job posting in the recruiter role, it might be a good idea to take a second look at it with these questions in mind.

Why is this relevant to you and the candidate?

On the company side, evaluating or screening candidates against the job profile leads to your initial decision about who could be a good fit and who is not. You need this screening process to narrow down the number of applicants to those you want to invite. It also allows you to start thinking about the questions you would ask them in an interview. Of course, the assessment will also help you determine which candidates to reject and why (see step 9 for more information on rejecting applicants).

Don't forget that even with an excellent selection process, mistakes can happen. The only exception is if you have worked with someone before—then you should know their strengths and weaknesses. Life experience from working together is always better than any paper-and-pencil assessment or interview. That's why it can make sense to contact references—other people who have worked with a candidate before—if you're unsure about a particular candidate. It is great if you can provide context and good intentions when speaking with a referee—in this case, your support for both parties, to make a win-win decision. If your referee senses your good intentions, you will be rewarded with helpful candidate insight.

Diligent candidates will also research the company that wants to hire them and then, of course, try to show in their application that they are a good fit for the open position. It may also be a good idea for candidates to ask company representatives during interviews why they think they're a good fit for the job and why they decided to interview them (so as a recruiter, you'd better have an answer for these questions prepared).

Steps 7 and 8: Interviewing and testing candidates

We've already come quite a long way in the recruitment process, to steps seven and eight out of twelve. Now that we've decided on a few candidates, it's time to dig deeper and find out if the candidate and the company are really a good fit.

You can also use recruitment tests for this purpose. When I talk about a recruitment test, I mean a specific procedure that requires applicants to fill out a form (e.g., a personality test) or perform tasks to assess what specific skills or personal traits they possess (e.g., intelligence). I recommend using tests when you have a lot of applicants, to filter out the most suitable ones. The downside is that you may reject candidates who have great personalities and are quick learners but do not yet possess the specific skills you need. You can also use tests in addition to a personal interview to get a more holistic picture of a candidate.

The advantage of tests is that you have a standardized set of questions that each candidate must answer. But it's also important to be aware of the potential drawbacks of using tests. For example, skills tests can be trained for. And personality tests pretend to make valid statements about a very complex topic using the answers to only a few questions (and some applicants might also try to give "desired" answers instead of honest ones). That's why I don't see tests as a panacea, but rather as a complement to human assessment.

One of the most commonly used assessment tools in recruitment is the job interview. When I talk about a job interview, I always mean a structured face-to-face interview. "Structured" means that the interview is based on the job description and job requirements.

It also means that the interview should be well prepared in advance.

A job interview typically includes:

1. a warm-up phase;
2. a phase in which the company representatives ask questions of the candidate;
3. a phase in which the candidate asks questions (the order of 2 and 3 can be changed or 2 and 3 can be intertwined); and
4. a phase where you discuss the next steps in the process.

So, as a recruiter, what is the best way to prepare for the job interview? First of all, it is important to understand that there are no "perfect" questions—there are only great answers (and some worse ones, of course). What is a helpful question for one candidate may not be helpful at all for another. A great interview is not the one where the interviewer asks the best questions—it is the one where, in a great atmosphere, relevant information is revealed on both sides.

In my experience, the best atmosphere for an interview is a bit like having coffee and chatting with friends, where you are curious to learn more about each other. Genuine curiosity to learn more about the other person is the key to success! However, there is a big difference from having coffee with friends: In a job interview, you should stick to specific topics (those that are highly relevant to the job) and, more importantly, you should never be curious about very intimate topics. You also need to ensure that you respect the laws of your country.

It is very important for both sides to ask open-ended questions that invite the other side to reveal a lot about themselves. I am often asked if the interviewer should avoid closed questions. Well, if you just bombard the candidate with open-ended questions, it can feel like a police interrogation. The flow of the interview is smoother and gentler when different types of questions bring a different rhythm into play. After an open-ended question such as *"How would you describe your resilience?"* it might be helpful to summarize what you, as the interviewer, understood from the answer and then ask, *"Did I understand that correctly?"* This is a closed question, but it will certainly do no harm. Be careful with leading questions during the interview, however. You should not give or suggest an answer, as this will not give you any new insight into the candidate.

If you have asked an open-ended question, it is important to interpret the answers well. For example, you might ask, *"What kind of leader are you?"* You may get what you think is an excellent answer from the candidate, but what does that answer really tell you? What did you learn about the candidate? It may be much more than their perception of their own leadership style. You may have learned that the candidate is quick-witted or confident—or that the candidate is nervous. If the main reason for asking this question was really to learn more about the candidate's leadership style, you could use follow-up questions to peel back the onion and get to the core (e.g., *"What exactly do you do that makes you a great leader?"*)

One of the main techniques that I use here is the STAR method.[5] STAR is an acronym for Situation, Task, Action, and Results. And I've added the "L." The STARL method is pretty simple to follow:

- *"Can you give me an example of a difficult leadership situation?"* (S)
- *"What exactly did you do?"* (T)
- *"How did you behave in that situation?"* (A)
- *"What was the result of your behavior?"* (R)
- *"And what have you learned from this situation?"* (L)

Really strong candidates (the "stars") give you STAR answers before you even ask for them.

Ideally, before you ask questions, you should know why you are asking them. The answer should lie in the job profile, the job requirements, and the "magic moments." And you should have a sense of what you would consider a strong or weak answer from the candidate. This will help you gauge the candidate and know what to ask next.

Some job interviews are incredibly boring because the same questions are asked over and over again (classic examples are questions like *"Where do you see yourself in five years?"* and *"What are your main strengths and weaknesses?"*). Good interviewers avoid asking generic questions that aren't specifically tailored to the candidate or the job profile. They also remain mindful that focusing too heavily on criteria can lead to missing valuable insights about the candidate that may emerge between the lines.

I always recommend that both recruiters and candidates take notes during the interview. This can help you absorb the information and allow you to make a more objective assessment after the interview. On the company side, you will usually base your evaluation on a set of prioritized criteria (on a priority scale of 1 to 3, with 1 being the highest priority) on which you can then rate the candidates (see an example in Table 4.1). I recommend using both numerical and behavioral assessments for all criteria. For the numerical rating, I use the following scale: 0=not at all met, 1=partially met, 2=met, 3=exceeds, 4=strongly exceeds.

Criteria	Detailed criteria	Priority	Candidate evaluation (0-4)	Evaluation (observation)
Teamwork	• Knows how to create a team spirit	2	4	The candidate used three great examples to illustrate how she effectively created bonds between people in new teams.
	• Connects across diverse opinions	2		
	• Finds win-win positions	1		

Table 4.1 An example of assessing one candidate on one assessment criterion

Why is this relevant to you and the candidate?

A structured assessment process increases objectivity and fairness by using standardized criteria and reducing the impact of personal bias. It also allows for a more reliable comparison of candidates, leading to more informed hiring decisions based on a consistent assessment framework. Being well prepared for the interview also allows you to get more relevant answers from candidates. If you are not sure what to look for in a candidate, you may need to take a step back and clearly define the job requirements and "magic moments" first. After all, your goal is to understand the candidate's preferences, attitudes, behaviors, and skills and how they overlap with the requirements and challenges of the job you are interviewing for (with the potential to create "magic moments" in that job).

For candidates, it is important to really understand the information in the job profile first in order to be able to prepare well for the assessment and selection process. The way that the company organizes this process (and how candidates are treated personally throughout it) also conveys valuable information to candidates. It's an important display of the company's values and will give candidates a sense of whether a company "walks the talk."

Steps 9 and 10: Rejecting applicants and deciding for new employees

This part of the process is perhaps the most underestimated. In many companies, rejecting candidates is seen as a routine nuisance that does not add value. But you can look at it differently, as an important way to communicate with people who may not be the best fit for the role you are currently offering, but who may come back as your customers, suppliers, or candidates for other roles for which they would be a much better fit. Remember, you'll meet people more than once in life, and next time you may be the one who needs the support of a former candidate.

Everyone who applies for an open position makes an effort and expects to receive feedback. As a recruiter, you should have a supportive attitude and always try to do your best to help candidates understand your decision. If you are not sure how to communicate, just follow the golden rule: Do unto others as you would have them do unto you. If you were rejected, what would you like to hear (and what would you not like to hear)?

Yes, of course, in recruitment "there can only be one" at a time.[6] But remember that everyone who applied for your job is also eager to learn and grow, and to be treated respectfully as a human being. So, try to be as open and personal as possible when giving the candidate feedback about your decision. Finally, framing the rejection in a way that the candidate can benefit from is also an employer branding opportunity. If candidates give you praise even though you did not offer them a job, consider yourself lucky to have just won first place in the recruiter's league!

Of course, after an effective assessment and selection process, the "one and only," the candidate you have decided to make an offer to, should also be excited about the next phases, negotiation and onboarding. And if you have done a good job in hiring, you can use the reasons why you chose the candidate (and their strengths) as a basis for their further development. And you can put their weaknesses aside for review or observation if they could potentially have a negative impact on their day-to-day work.

What are the benefits for applicants and companies in phases 9 and 10? The key advantage is gaining a clear understanding of why a candidate advanced to the next stage or didn't. Both parties should feel positive about these steps. Receiving constructive and supportive factual and emotional feedback is important for both sides.

Why is this relevant to you and the candidate?

When companies are respectful, responsive, and clear in their feedback to all applicants, including those who are ultimately selected, it creates a reputation as an employer that is better than any employer branding consultant's concept could ever achieve. When feedback comes from a deep desire to help people develop and grow, whether they are candidates you have to reject or your future employees, they will reward this with kudos, likes, long service, or that all-important positive word-of-mouth, which can be a huge advantage for your company in a tight labor market.

Step 11: Negotiating with candidates

For the selected candidate, the next step is also very important. The way you negotiate their contract will tell them which of their skills will be rewarded and how. It's also a phase where they can still jump ship, so make sure you get it right.

Most companies see reward and recognition as an important step in retaining employees. Salary levels are usually determined by a number of factors: legal requirements, an assessment of the value added by a job, performance, and a market assessment of skills and competencies, both within your company (the "internal salary market") and in the broader labor market.

You will typically ask what employees earn in their current job and what they expect from their new job, and then try to match that with your budget possibilities to find a solution that meets the needs of both sides. Attractive employers are also not afraid to enter into a negotiation process even if the outcome may be that the financial expectations simply do not match. Sometimes financial negotiations require a lot of creativity and patience to meet both parties' expectations. If the candidate's expectations exceed the company's budget for that particular position, there are a few options that can be explored:

- Option 1: The candidate receives a starting salary that is slightly below their expectations, but a guaranteed increase based on performance or results in the first six months on the job.
- Option 2: The candidate receives a first-year bonus based on certain performance criteria (parts of the first-year bonus may even be fixed).
- Option 3: A percentage of the salary increase is locked in for the next annual salary review.

One of the most common mistakes in the negotiation phase is that the prospective employer does not take the time to listen carefully to the candidate and does not ask questions, but rushes through the process with the motto "We have the finalist now, let's get them to sign!" It is also not a good idea to focus the negotiations exclusively on money. Don't forget the importance of all the other elements that attracted the candidate in the first place ("magic moments" on the job, development opportunities, a great boss, or an exciting product).

Why is this relevant to you and the candidate?

During the negotiation process, the recruiter learns more about the prospective employee and how they think and feel about rewards and recognition. If done in a way that is sensitive to the candidate's concerns, the negotiation process can also strengthen the bond that has already been established during the recruitment process. Sometimes an intense negotiation process has aired and resolved many issues. And of course, if the negotiation is done well, you will have a committed new employee on board who is happy with the overall package and the job they are taking on.

The negotiation process gives candidates a sense of how they will be involved and treated in difficult conversations. It also gives them a sense of whether the employer is really willing to invest time, money, and effort to find a win-win solution. Ideally, they will be satisfied with the whole process and the outcome for them—and with their new job.

Step 12: Onboarding

The last phase of the recruitment process is also the first phase at the beginning of an employee's life cycle. The onboarding phase can last anywhere from three months to about a year.

In my own recruitment agency, onboarding is as much a part of our service as helping in the earlier stages of the recruitment process. New challenges can arise during the onboarding phase, and we can quickly bring any issues to the surface—and then help resolve them—through ongoing conversations with the new employee and the employer.

The general idea of onboarding is to provide newly hired employees with the relevant knowledge and network from day one, saving them the time (and therefore the company's money) it would take to figure it all out on their own. There's a lot of variation in how companies handle the onboarding phase. For example, it can include mentoring, special training programs, or boot camps where new employees have the opportunity to network and experience the company culture firsthand.

Typically, companies invest a great deal of time and energy in recruiting and believe they've been successful by the time the contract is signed. However, if they do not show new recruits the respect they deserve by helping them integrate, they run the risk of creating a high turnover of new employees. This can also jeopardize the culture the company wants to build. Onboarding is therefore not only an investment in employee performance and motivation but also in creating and maintaining a great culture.

When is a candidate sufficiently onboarded? It's a question I'm often asked by my clients, and my answer is simple: when they are performing well and enjoying their work, and have found colleagues or sparring partners they enjoy collaborating with.

Why is this relevant to you and the candidate?

Considering onboarding as an integral part of the recruitment process is very important if you want to get highly motivated, well-integrated, and high-performing employees with a strong network. Like the careful design and execution of the rest of the recruiting process, it is an investment, but one that can pay off for everyone.

DEVELOP YOUR RECRUITING SKILLS

Reflecting on your recruitment process

1. Honestly, which of the steps in your recruiting process are really well thought out in terms of how they benefit both the company and the candidate?
2. What is the strongest part of your recruitment process? What differentiates you from your competitors? And how could you make it even better?
3. Which steps could you improve (and in what way)?
4. Do you know what candidates think of your process (ideally, each step in the process)? Consider sending out a survey to 30 (great) candidates to find out.
5. What are your key takeaways from the answers to questions 1 to 4? Based on your findings, create a concrete improvement plan.

The role of technology: How AI can help you recruit the best team

This chapter provides a nuanced perspective on how technology—particularly artificial intelligence (AI)—can help you build the best team. There are pros and cons regarding the use of technology and its effectiveness in supporting different steps in the recruiting process. Our focus here is on the usefulness of technology in addressing specific recruiting challenges.

In the previous chapter, we examined the twelve steps of the recruitment process and how they can best be organized to create value for both candidates and employers. In this chapter, we will explore the role that technology can play in the recruitment process, focusing on where it can truly add value (and not just be a "nice-to-have" addition).

So, what do I mean when I talk about the role that technology can play in recruitment? With the advent of generative AI, the question is what impact it will have on recruitment. On the one hand, I believe we are in for significant advances, but on the other hand, we need to keep a close eye on what this technology is really contributing to recruitment outcomes. AI is definitely a new player in recruitment, but we don't yet know exactly how it will change the entire field. Therefore, I propose a thought experiment that focuses on the results that will be achieved with and without this new technology.

Overall, I intuitively believe that we, as humans, should view technology as a collaborative partner in recruitment. This means that we need to identify who has what strengths in different hiring situations in order to optimize the entire recruitment process. For example, when it comes to analyzing a large amount of candidate data to find the person with the most experience in a particular field, technology ("the machine" or algorithm) is much faster than any human recruiter when you have 200 candidates to sift through. However, when it comes to reading between the lines and determining, for example, which of those 200 candidates might be a good fit for a different position, the human is—at least at the time of writing this book—still better at recognizing various aspects of the résumés that AI might miss.

You can compare AI to a computer that can beat any chess player but lacks the free will to decide that it would rather play table tennis than chess. While the technology is excellent in terms of speed and data processing, it currently lacks the ability to analyze human data from an emotional perspective and make decisions like a human. AI is designed to limit variability, not expand it.

What is new about generative AI? Unlike a search engine, it works as a "reasoning engine." It interprets your input—whether spoken or written—and creates new content based on the data or prompt you provide. It reacts dynamically, not statically, and can learn from your questions or prompts in real time. Generative AI creates content using probability methods, calculating the most likely correct answer. However, this also (currently) means that the answer may still be wrong or "hallucinated." Over time, with improved data quality and refined prompts, the accuracy of AI's calculations will increase.

In other words, generative AI is an area of artificial intelligence that uses algorithms and models to create new content based on existing data. It uses machine learning to identify patterns and structures in the data and then generates new content that follows these patterns.

So, what does all this mean for recruiting? Let me discuss the value of recruitment technology through three guiding questions:

1. How can we—as humans—still be useful in recruiting the best people in the face of rapid technological progress?
2. How can the collaboration between "the machine" and human recruiters be optimized?
3. How can we objectively and critically evaluate AI without fear?

The intelligent use of AI in recruitment

In general, I believe it's beneficial to approach innovation in recruitment (as in other business-related areas) with a clear understanding of the problem you're trying to solve or the benefit you're trying to create. AI is no different than any other technological solution you have implemented in your business. Just focus on the following two questions:

1. What problem can a new solution or technology solve for you?
2. What outcome will it improve?

Focusing on the solution and outcomes rather than on the process can help you decide when and where to use AI in recruiting. If you ask me, simply following the hype will not get you or your company anywhere. On the other hand, if there is an outcome for you in the hype, don't miss it.

If you have many job openings and receive a large number of applications, you can use a résumé parsing tool. It structures all résumés in a consistent format, providing the same length and information for each, which can improve efficiency and help reduce bias.[1] However, the originality of the candidate can be lost in the process. And the concept is not new; LinkedIn has offered such a parsing tool for years.

If you have a large candidate database, a matching tool that compares the job criteria with the résumé data can be very helpful. However, this approach is not new either; it is essentially what

Google and LinkedIn algorithms have been doing for decades—matching search criteria with data in a database. For example, if you search for a certain type of candidate, LinkedIn will suggest new candidates based on those skills. The algorithm learns from your approval or rejection of the suggested candidates. This technology has been around for years, so there's nothing particularly new on the horizon in this regard.

What is relatively new is that AI can now write personalized emails and ask candidates personalized questions. A 2023 US study found that about 50 percent of people could not distinguish human language from machine-generated language.[2] Human judgments were based on intuitive but flawed heuristics, such as speech contractions and the use of first-person pronouns. This suggests that it will soon be difficult to distinguish between machine and human communication, creating a new level of competition in reaching passive candidates.

Until now, a highly personalized approach required a deep understanding of the candidate's profile, meaning recruiters had to familiarize themselves with the candidate to achieve a higher response rate than other recruiters. This advantage may be eroded by AI. The question remains whether further steps, such as the initial interview, will also be handled by "the machine" with the same level of personalization and human touch. We may be approaching that point soon.

I recently listened to a podcast where ChatGPT was asked about the future of hiring.[3] I have to admit that, aside from the tone of voice, the frequent repetition of statements, and the awkward response to humor, the machine's arguments had a human touch. For example, ChatGPT argued that it could never fully replace a human recruiter because of the psychological understanding required to read between the lines and interpret body language. The AI acknowledged its strengths and its role in helping recruiters work more effectively, but emphasized that successful matchmaking still requires human decision-making and judgment. This perspective echoed my own thoughts and those of many of my colleagues about how machines and humans can work together to achieve the best outcome—finding the right candidate for a particular job based on their talents and aspirations. In the end, ChatGPT offered the same conclusion that I would have come to: Let's focus on what we know and do best!

What I currently see on LinkedIn is a good attempt at writing personalized messages, but it still lacks what I would call a human touch. While the machine recruiter is able to connect the dots, it does not yet generate the feelings that can engage people, spark their curiosity, and ideally motivate candidates to respond. I learned from LinkedIn that my own response rate for LinkedIn outreach is extremely high at around 49 percent, compared to a typical high response rate of around 38 percent. It remains to be seen whether "the machine" will be able to achieve similar response rates.

I leave it to you to judge for yourself what you think of the human touch in machine-generated messages. Let's take the example of me as a recruiter on LinkedIn writing a message to myself as a candidate (yes, this can be done—the system allowed me to send such a message without worrying about the possible connection between me and myself).

So here is the message that LinkedIn's AI function generated for me:

> Hi Barbara,
>
> Warm greetings! My name is Barbara, a [sic!] Advisor at PKF C&P Business Development GmbH. I saw your profile and was impressed by your professional experience.
>
> I noticed that you are currently working as an Advisor at PKF C&P Business Development GmbH. Our shared connections on LinkedIn have encouraged me to reach out and learn more about your professional goals.

> We have a full-time opportunity at PKF C&P Business Development GmbH for an Advisor. If you'd like to discuss this further, please let me know when you're available for a call.
>
> Best regards
> Barbara

Let's look at a second example (after all, you probably won't recruit yourself too often). The next outreach is for my publisher, Dietmar. Unfortunately, the LinkedIn system does not yet allow you to change the role or topic of your outreach. In the outreach below, it just suggests a role to Dietmar based on his LinkedIn profile, without any connection to our open roles:

> Hi Dietmar,
>
> Good day! I am from PKF C&P Business Development GmbH, and your profile and background really stood out.
>
> We have a full-time job opening at PKF C&P Business Development GmbH for the position of Founder, CEO and Publisher. Your experience as a Founder, CEO and Publisher at econcise might be relevant for this role.
>
> Our common connections on LinkedIn indicate your interest in our company and encouraged me to share this opportunity with you.
>
> I would be happy to provide more details about this position over a call if it sounds like a potential fit.
>
> Best regards
> Barbara

In my opinion, this contradicts the study mentioned above because it is immediately obvious that this message is not really personalized and was either generated by a machine or is a mass mail. However, a recruiter could use the tool to see what kind of role the AI would suggest to the candidate. In the case above, the suggested role—taken verbatim from my publisher's profile—obviously makes no sense at all.

Of course, this is only where things stand as I am writing this book. AI-based systems will certainly continue to advance rapidly, at LinkedIn and elsewhere.

I would compare the evolution of recruiting technology to other significant technological advances throughout history. Just as the automobile replaced the carriage and the cell phone replaced the landline, technological advances have always had a profound impact on business and society.

My experience with ChatGPT and similar AI-powered tools suggests that we should view them as assistants or partners that excel at quickly digesting large amounts of data. We need to learn to collaborate and work effectively with this new technology for the benefit of our clients and candidates. In recruiting, these tools can be extremely helpful in creating job profiles, interview guidelines, corporate target lists, job advertisements, and outreach texts, keeping in mind the limitations we discussed above. They can also help develop recruiting strategies, perhaps even creating slides or videos that recruiters can use to pitch to their managers.

Recently, I have enjoyed using a platform called TLDV (*https://tldv.io*), which summarizes interviews or calls on video conferencing platforms such as Zoom and Google Meet. It can also analyze interviews, a feature that is already being used to evaluate candidates and as a learning opportunity for both recruiters and candidates. As I write this book, Microsoft is testing similar technology, and other vendors have come out with their own solutions.

For experienced HR managers, "the machine" can be a great help. However, for the inexperienced, there is a significant risk of missing the "hallucinations" or mistakes that AI can generate (similar to mistakes made by a colleague or boss). Therefore, we should also recognize our responsibility as experienced recruiters to teach inexperienced colleagues how to use these new AI tools effectively.

In my teaching, I have also noticed that the students who think critically before using AI tools achieve excellent results and learn a lot with the help of AI. However, if they use AI without engaging their own critical thinking, they will not work effectively with the technology. While the machine learns with every prompt, humans do not learn when they type without thinking. As a result, the quality of the prompts may not improve and humans may become too dependent on the machine.

This is the big risk I see with the use of AI in recruitment—when people rely on it without the life experience and knowledge needed to use the tools in a truly intelligent way. I am aware that I may sound a bit old-fashioned here, but I am convinced that an effective collaboration between humans and "the machine" will still outperform AI alone for some time to come. Human expertise will continue to be in demand when it comes to hiring people, also because people will, at least for the time being, still want to rely on a decision made by other people.

All in all, AI is undoubtedly a wave in recruitment that you will want to ride to stay ahead of the competition. However, always keep an eye on the bottom line and honestly assess whether using AI will improve the results of your process steps before making the decision to use "the machine" in your recruiting efforts.

Using AI in the individual steps of the recruitment process

Let us now examine the potential benefits of using AI in the various stages of the recruitment process (see Chapter 4), as well as areas where caution is needed.

Recruitment step 1: Creating a need

Benefits: How can you use your historical data combined with AI probability calculations to predict future hiring needs for your team? By considering different needs and scenarios, you can better prepare your hiring strategies. AI excels at combining data, which it can do much more effectively than humans.

Watch out: Be wary of AI-generated "hallucinations." Make sure you interpret the data sensibly, for example by involving colleagues and using different AI tools.

Recruitment steps 2–5: Describing the job, its requirements, and its "magic moments," and promoting the job

Benefits: How can you use AI as a buddy, colleague, friend, or assistant to deliver better content? If you're an expert in the field, AI can save you time by generating new, well-written content that you might not have thought of, and even translating it into different languages.

Watch out: If you're not already well-versed in these recruiting topics, keep an open mind and critically evaluate the results you get from AI. Think carefully before using "the machine," and discuss the content with colleagues and job holders to ensure your results remain diverse. One of the biggest criticisms of AI is that it can limit the variability of the answers it provides.

Recruitment steps 6–8: Screening résumés and interviewing, testing, and assessing candidates

Benefits: AI can handle large volumes of résumés, bring them into a standardized format, and remove portrait photos to reduce human bias. It can help narrow down the pool to candidates with similar competencies and analyze candidate performance in video interviews from a more "objective" perspective. In addition, AI can assist in reaching out to candidates with personalized messages.

Watch out: Acceptance of AI in more communicative stages, such as interviews, remains uncertain. Candidates may prefer companies that use human colleagues for these steps. In addition, while AI can help develop assessment methods, candidates—especially in technical fields—might also use AI to excel in these assessments. Be aware of candidates who might be better prepared with AI assistance.

Recruitment step 10: Deciding for a candidate

Benefits: AI can help you draw the right conclusions by indicating which candidate it would prefer based on data analysis.

Watch out: I strongly believe that the final decision for a candidate should and will be made by a human being. Believing in the candidate you choose is critical to a successful working relationship. And just imagine, if there were challenges or problems after the hiring process, who would you turn to for a re-evaluation of the hire—the machine that made the decision? Another machine?

Recruitment step 11: Negotiating with candidates

Benefits: AI can help you calculate different scenarios based on the company's salary data and external salary benchmarks. It can also help predict how the candidate might react to different offers. Ask "the machine" to assume different preferences of the candidate and enter them into the prompt.

Watch out: Negotiations are similar to interviews, where human interaction is highly valued. Use AI to analyze and calculate scenarios, but rely on your instincts and judgment to choose the best negotiation strategy. You can use "the machine" to gather input, but the final approach should be human-driven.

Recruitment step 12: Onboarding

Benefits: With the increasing use of AI and chatbots to effectively handle customer queries and resolve customer complaints, why not give every new hire their own personal chatbot buddy or mentor? This chatbot could refer them on to a human colleague if a question remains unanswered.

Watch out: While having an AI buddy could be fun and save human colleagues' time, the integration period is crucial for transferring cultural habits, product knowledge, company processes, and motivation to new employees. It's uncertain whether a chatbot can effectively transfer the motivational energy that human colleagues can provide.

In summary, there are exciting opportunities to improve the efficiency and effectiveness of the various steps in the recruitment process and create valuable outcomes through the use of AI. However, it is important to stay in the driver's seat and ensure human involvement where necessary to maintain a balance between efficiency and the irreplaceable value of human judgment and interaction. After all, we are recruiting humans, and we don't want to leave that task entirely to machines, do we?

DEVELOP YOUR RECRUITING SKILLS

Reflecting on the use of AI in the recruitment process

1. As you review your current recruiting process, where could AI potentially help improve results the most?
2. How ready and experienced are you and your staff (recruiters, managers, and colleagues) to use AI? What steps need to be taken to ensure you can effectively integrate AI as a valuable recruitment tool?

Recruitment is more than recruitment

This chapter provides an overview of strategies beyond talent acquisition that can help teams and organizations acquire specific skills. It is intended to encourage you to explore alternative approaches when traditional talent acquisition is not producing the desired results. Sometimes thinking outside the box is necessary to overcome your recruiting challenges.

In a highly competitive market for talent, acquiring the right skills often requires more than traditional recruitment methods. Fortunately, there are alternative strategies that can effectively fill skill gaps within teams and organizations. By exploring these innovative approaches, you can discover new solutions when traditional talent acquisition falls short.

Let's start with a brief overview of what you can do to grow or improve your team, whether in terms of increasing efficiency and effectiveness, motivation, or adding different and new skills.

- You can automate (and reorganize).
- You can hire temporary staff (e.g., interim management, freelancers, consultants).
- You can train and develop people.
- You can collaborate with different types of stakeholders (e.g., customers, suppliers, agents or intermediaries, educational institutions).

- You can outsource.
- You can buy a team or a company.

We will look at all of these approaches in more detail in this chapter. But this is by no means an exhaustive list, and I am sure you can think of other ways to access talent and skills. It pays to be creative—even when it comes to recruiting.

You can automate

When you think about automation as an alternative to hiring, here is the central question you should ask yourself: What tasks can "the machine" or an algorithm take over to free up valuable time for skilled employees?

Considering the potential limitations of AI that we discussed in Chapter 5 and the current discussion about where AI can be used, what kind of work in your sales, logistics, finance, R&D, or HR departments could be further automated? AI can be seen as part of the solution when it comes to creating more capacity and more manpower (or, in this particular case, "machine power").

The current discussion around AI supports the idea that the future of knowledge work can largely be transferred to intelligent algorithms. Examples include AI-driven customer service, inventory systems, and tools that help you become a better salesperson or recruiter, essentially acting as a coach. However, according to a recent study by the London-based Institute for Public Policy Research, it is primarily simple support and back-office work that can be easily automated—what the authors call the "low-hanging fruit" of AI.[1] AI can free your team members from monotonous or administrative tasks, allowing them to learn new skills and engage in more meaningful work that benefits the company. In an industry where finding good employees can be a challenge, this must be the ideal.

This can be a real win-win for you and your current employees, freeing them from unloved tasks and replacing them with meaningful and challenging work that fosters personal and professional growth. Of course, I am not a social romantic. I fully understand that for most organizations, automation is ultimately not about recruiting, but about long-term cost savings. So, of course, it still needs to be aligned with your business case. But if automation can benefit multiple areas—freeing people from tedious administrative work and saving money at the same time—it is even more ideal. The key point is that automation can inspire solutions to both your staffing and your business challenges, as long as you have clear outcomes in mind and are honest about what machines and algorithms can and cannot do (as discussed in Chapter 5).

You can hire temporary staff

Temporary staff—individuals hired on a short-term basis to meet immediate staffing needs without long-term commitments—are another alternative to recruiting full-time employees. Examples include freelancers, one-person contractors, interim managers, consultants, people hired through temporary employment agencies, and student workers. The key consideration when hiring temporary staff is determining what tasks are appropriate for them.

In general, hiring temporary staff follows the same principles of recruitment discussed throughout this book. Let me quickly recap a few thoughts.

Remember the key question related to the recruitment mindset—do you see the glass as half full or half empty? Are you hiring temporary staff just as a stopgap measure, or do you see it as an opportunity to meet and work with great people? Yes, these are people who have chosen a different work model and a different lifestyle. But keep in mind that they could potentially also work for you more than just once on a temporary basis. And you might also want to keep in mind the old adage that temporary solutions sometimes last longer than permanent ones.

A key characteristic of freelancers, consultants, and interim managers is that they are not permanently on your payroll; they work independently, through an intermediary, or for another organization that assigns them to your projects. Typically, you hire these professionals for projects with a defined timeline, scope, budget, and team, leading to a natural end to the contract. However, labor shortages and team constraints often extend the tenure of great freelancers. Sometimes these freelancers choose to join your team permanently, or they may move on to other clients to enhance their learning and spread their business risk.

I always advise my clients to build what I call a "flexible team" of temporary workers or helpers, such as a software developer or interim marketing manager, to cover for permanent employees on maternity or paternity leave, sabbatical, or long-term illness.

Some of my clients prefer to hire permanent rather than temporary employees for a variety of reasons. One reason is the traditional belief that employers have more control when employees are fully employed under their contract and rules, which also reflects a certain ("command and control") management style. However, in new industries such as online businesses, I often see the opposite approach, where the type of contract is much less important. Your personality and impact are much more important than the legal arrangement of your employment. Regardless of your general preference, don't overlook the freelance and temp industry—you can find great people there!

If you are still wary of hiring freelancers, remember that projects started out of necessity can sometimes lead to the best employees with full-time contracts. As described in Chapters 1 and 2, your attitude determines the opportunities you see—and this is true in different forms of recruiting. Don't forget that an entrepreneurial mindset is often a valued quality in new team members. The term "entrepreneurial" comes from the French word *"entreprendre,"* which means "to do something" or "to tackle something." People who dare to take risks as freelancers, and who are usually quite adept at tackling and successfully completing projects, tend to embody this trait. Finally, working together on a project is a great way to determine how well a freelancer will fit into your team.

You can upskill your team (educate from within)

The driving question behind training is: What competencies and behaviors do employees need to develop in order to effectively perform the future tasks of your organization?

You may be surprised that this book does not include a chapter on talent retention. This is because I believe that applying the mindset outlined in Chapter 1 also lays the foundation for retaining great people for the long term. Addressing business challenges such as labor shortages by developing internal employees through training and giving them opportunities to work in different roles and departments automatically encourages learning and growth. It also keeps your team members engaged. Most employees love to grow themselves and the business, and eating the sweet fruit that can be harvested from these seeds together with managers and owners provides satisfaction for everyone. This makes your team members valuable contributors at the table of success.

So what kind of training am I talking about? If a software developer wants to manage a project, they could, for example, get a project management coach or a project management buddy, or take a project management course. If a successful salesperson wants to become a leader, they can work with a leadership coach, be mentored by an internal manager, take a self-awareness seminar, or listen to an inspiring leadership podcast. If a recruiter wants to become a sales expert, they can read a book, attend a sales academy, or take on a small sales project to enhance their skills.

Of course, training is not free. It takes time, patience, and investment. A new skill needs to be practiced, and people need to learn from mistakes. And that takes time. Usually we seem to lack time, the most precious thing in our lives. Money is abundant, but time is not. It is limited, for you and me, for the President of the United States, for the King and Queen of England, and for your team member. And we must also remember that not everything can be learned by everyone. Learning something new takes will and persistence, motivation and courage. And sometimes also technical skills.

You can collaborate with others or outsource

The central question in collaboration is: What tasks can a partner perform to deliver a joint product or service? A collaboration partner can be anyone who provides part of your service to your (joint) customer. The end product can be an existing one, or you can also create something new with your partner.

The key question in outsourcing is: Who can do some of your work better, cheaper, or faster than you can, so that you can deliver a superior product or service to your customers in a cost-effective way?

Collaboration and outsourcing are slightly different concepts. Collaboration is when two partners work together to provide a service, while outsourcing is when one partner performs work for another. But the difference is nuanced.

The general logic behind both approaches is similar to that of recruiting: first you need to define the partner's tasks and required skills. Whether you are collaborating to create something new or outsourcing some of your work, you need to understand each other's values, behaviors, history, expectations, and roles in order to be successful (see Chapter 2). The next step is to develop a plan that defines exactly who needs to do what within a specific time frame. It seems so logical, and perhaps even boring, to point this out, yet it so often goes wrong.

When I worked for a semiconductor company, it was common knowledge that when software became as important as hardware in a microchip, hardware-oriented semiconductor companies would partner with software vendors in the early stages to develop a chip with more software functionality. It was the lack of knowledge and understanding of software that drove the semiconductor companies to seek partnerships.

The process of finding the right partner or supplier for the long term is very similar to the hiring process described in the earlier chapters of this book. There may be a greater degree of complexity because it is a B2B relationship that typically involves more people, but remember that, just as with people, your partner's values and story must align with your company's values. This alignment is the foundation for a successful long-term collaboration or outsourcing relationship.

Start by clarifying the service (service description) and profiling the partner you are looking for. It can also be helpful to specify what you are not looking for in a partner. Finally, create your own story about why a partner should be interested in collaborating with you.

You can buy a team or company

There are two key questions to consider when buying an entire team: How do you scale a particular skill set by buying or hiring more than one person? And: How do you successfully integrate the acquired company into your organization?

Hand on heart, what company focused on AI development would not buy a team of 10 AI developers right now if they had the funds? Investing in a team speeds up the process of integrating new people and skills into your team compared to hiring individuals one at a time. Also, buying a team means buying an existing set of (hopefully) well-functioning working relationships.

The critical relationship to develop first is between you—the buyer—and the acquired team. In addition to building the relationship, it is essential to align or integrate processes, such as, in the AI development example above, the software development process. Successful integration can result in a synergy where 1+1=3; poor integration will almost certainly result in significantly less than 2.

When hiring teams or buying companies, the buyer often believes that their way of doing things will outperform the acquired team. But why did they buy the team in the first place? I do not want to delve too deeply into the M&A process (that would require a book on its own), but I find this point crucial because I have experienced it myself. When the buyer feels "superior" to the acquired team, it stifles collaboration. This can lead to a dynamic where the new team members withhold effort and ideas, a common post-merger problem that is often overlooked. I have seen this happen several times. When the buying company insists that the acquired team must adopt its methods, it wastes time, energy, and money. However, if the buyer is willing to review processes with the acquired team and create a new way of working together—one that can outperform the competition—they will succeed. Treating the new team as equals and including them in discussions will foster their commitment to collective success.

Before deciding to buy another company, review the people on the team, their values, processes, salaries, benefits, and the results the team has produced over the past few years. Conduct thorough business and market due diligence, but do not forget cultural due diligence. You may also want to consider consulting with an M&A professional whose values align with yours.

For larger companies, there is also the option of inviting startups into internal scale-up programs to drive innovation and business development—or to have access to great people and teams if the innovation doesn't work out as planned.

Acquiring a team is more complex, time-consuming, and investment-intensive than hiring one employee at a time. It also requires a lot of preparation and post-acquisition integration work and skills. On the other hand, it is certainly an option worth exploring if you need to hire a large number of people with specific skills at once.

Find your own creative way to recruit your team

I hope this chapter has given you some new perspectives on how to close the skills gap in your organization. There are many roads to Rome—even in recruiting. Which one you choose depends on your pain point, the urgency of your recruiting needs, and the resources that are available to you. The list presented here is not exhaustive. Maybe you can think of other ways to recruit? Then I would love to hear from you!

DEVELOP YOUR RECRUITING SKILLS

Reflecting on alternative forms of recruitment

Reviewing your current recruiting approaches:

1. What has worked well for you in your current approaches to recruiting?
2. What has not worked for you?

Considering new approaches:

3. Of the alternative recruiting approaches presented in this chapter, which approach might be interesting for your organization, and why?
4. What are the risks and opportunities for your business if you try one of these approaches?

Learning from others:

5. What organizations around you (in your industry, in your area, where your friends work) have successfully tried alternative recruiting approaches?
6. What did they do and how did they succeed?

A concluding note

It's a great honor for me that you've made it to this page.
I hope you enjoyed the journey and feel confident and inspired to become a great leader in recruitment.

I hope you've picked up a few valuable recruitment insights.

I hope you're still curious, but now with a deeper understanding.

I hope you feel refreshed and ready to take the next step in your recruitment process.

I sincerely hope you'll share your experiences, thoughts, feedback, or any inspiration you've gained along the way with me (see my contact details below).

* * *

As we reach the end of this book, let me briefly recap a few key points of our journey:

In Chapter 1, I tried to give you some **new perspectives on recruiting**. The aim was to inspire you to see recruiting as deeply connected to sales, investment, leadership, and more, and to highlight the nuances of this important activity beyond a purely process-driven approach.

In Chapter 2, I encouraged you to **explore your business story**—an authentic narrative about who you are and how you work—as a foundation for attracting talented people and other stakeholders to your organization.

The aim of Chapter 3 was to give you a step-by-step guide to **aligning your story with the needs and expectations of your stakeholders**, whether they are investors, customers, employees, or others. The key takeaway: Start with your story, then consider the expectations of others.

Chapter 4 summarized the **critical steps in the hiring process**, emphasizing how this process can serve both you and the candidate. The goal was to present the process as a tool that can benefit both parties.

In Chapter 5, we explored the **role of technology and AI in recruiting**, focusing on how these tools can truly benefit your efforts and not just be a "hot topic."

Finally, in Chapter 6, we explored **alternative strategies for addressing your recruiting needs**, offering different approaches to help you build your best team.

And what if you have hired the wrong person, even though you have done your best or followed some of the principles discussed in this book? Just admit it. Discuss it with other managers or key stakeholders. Don't stick to a decision that destroys value in your organization.

The most effective way to deal with someone who just doesn't fit is to let them go. Yes, you may have made the wrong decision. Unfortunately, it happens—you are also human! But you always have the choice to recognize the mistake, address it, and correct it.

If you found the content of this book thought-provoking and valuable—and feel that this book could be useful to others who are looking for the "right match," I would be very grateful if you would help spread the word by posting an honest online review. Not only will your feedback be valuable to me as an author, but it could also help others discover valuable insights that could make a real difference to their recruitment journey.

Finally, I'd like to leave you with a few questions to ponder:
- What inspired you in this book?
- What ideas do you feel compelled to try?
- Where do you want to build on my thoughts and ideas?
- Where do you disagree, or even feel frustrated by any of the ideas or statements presented?
- What would you like to add?

Feel free to get in touch: email me at *office@barbara-stampf.at* or send me a LinkedIn message at *https://www.linkedin.com/in/barbara-stampf-81610029/*

I look forward to hearing from you! And if you would like to present my thoughts and experiences in your company, feel free to contact me as well.

This book ends here, but new experiences are already on the horizon. As one door closes, another opens.

* * *

I wish you growth through the challenges of recruiting.

I wish you a healthy and fulfilling journey
in recruitment and beyond.

May you find the right match,
and may your dreams come true.

All the best
Barbara

Endnotes

Introduction

[1] Nyad, D. (2013). Never, ever give up [TED talk]. https://www.ted.com/talks/diana_nyad_never_ever_give_up, accessed 21 August 2024.

Chapter 1 Recruitment comes in different shades

[1] Chamberlain A., & Zhao, D. (2019). The key to happy customers? Happy employees. https://hbr.org/2019/08/the-key-to-happy-customers-happy-employees, accessed 26 April 2023; De Mol, E. (2019). What makes a successful startup team. https://hbr.org/2019/03/what-makes-a-successful-startup-team, accessed 26 April 2023.

[2] This is not just true for the most talented recruits. Research in sports shows that, on average, the team with the best player in a basketball league wins the league only 15 percent of the time (similar results are found in the movie industry). See Ulrich D. et al. (2017). *Victory Through Organization: Why the War for Talent is Failing Your Company and What You Can Do About It*. New York, NY: McGraw Hill Professional, pp. 55–79.

[3] Ulrich, D. (1996). *Human Resources Champion: The Next Agenda for Adding Value and Delivering Results*. Boston, MA: Harvard Business School Press, pp. 24–25.

[4] Hopkins, I. (2015). Dave Ulrich exclusive: CEO succession – are you ready for the top job? https://www.hcamag.com/au/specialisation/leadership/dave-ulrich-exclusive-ceo-succession-are-you-ready-for-the-top-job/142108, accessed 30 April 2023.

[5] Sinek, S. (2019). *The Infinite Game*. New York, NY: Penguin.

[6] By the way, I strongly believe that provocative questions that take you out of your comfort zone—like the one my student asked—are a wonderful learning opportunity, whether they come from students, customers, partners, colleagues, or children. If someone provokes you with a question, try not to take it too personally, but rather see it as a chance to learn. You will surely notice the difference between being blocked by negative emotions such as fear, anger, or anxiety, and approaching such situations with a mixture of curiosity, trust, and joy, which is the basis for learning, especially outside your comfort zone.

[7] Lambert, L. (2024). How a mission to cut food waste launched a multimillion-dollar venture. https://hbswk.hbs.edu/item/how-a-mission-to-cut-food-waste-launched-a-multimillion-dollar-venture, accessed 9 August 2024.

[8] Rosenthal, R., & Jacobson, L. (1968). Pygmalion in the classroom. *The Urban Review*, 3(1), 16–20.

[9] Yeager, D. S., Carroll, J. M., Buontempo, J., Cimpian, A., Woody, S., Crosnoe, R., ... & Dweck, C. S. (2022). Teacher mindsets help explain where a growth-mindset intervention does and doesn't work. *Psychological Science*, 33(1), 18–32.

[10] Houston, M. (2021). The art or caring leadership in business can increase ROI. https://www.forbes.com/sites/melissahouston/2021/06/16/the-art-of-caring-leadership-in-business-can-increase-roi/?sh=46f7e2422dad, accessed 23 March 2023.

Chapter 2 Recruitment tells a story

[1] Although I have a deep insight into the company, I want to emphasize that this is my personal view of the history of snigel.com up to 2023.

Chapter 3 Recruitment is an "inside-out" job (or why employer branding should come last)

[1] Mahajan, N. (2019). Human resources should focus on delivering value outside their companies (interview with Dave Ulrich). https://www.rolandberger.com/en/Insights/Publications/Dave-Ulrich-on-the-outside-in-view-of-HR.html, accessed 27 April 2023.

[2] Elements #1–#3 are based on Aristotle's teaching on how to convince other people (see Braet, A. C. (1992). Ethos, pathos and logos in Aristotle's Rhetoric: A re-examination. *Argumentation, 6*, 307–320).

[3] House, R. J., Hanges, P. J., Javidan, M., Dorfman, P. W., & Gupta, V. (eds) (2004). *Culture, Leadership, and Organizations: The GLOBE Study of 62 Societies*. Thousand Oaks, CA: SAGE Publications.

[4] Edmondson, A. C. (2018). *The Fearless Organization: Creating Psychological Safety in the Workplace for Learning, Innovation, and Growth*. Hoboken, NJ: John Wiley & Sons.

[5] Elements #4, 5 and 6 are based on ideas in Pink, D. H. (2011). *Drive: The Surprising Truth About What Motivates Us*. New York, NY: Penguin/Riverhead Books.

[6] Shontell, A. (2016). A 69-year-old monk who scientists call the "world's happiest man" says the secret to being happy takes just 15 minutes a day. https://www.businessinsider.com/how-to-be-happier-according-to-matthieu-ricard-the-worlds-happiest-man-2016-1#:~:text=Matthieu%20Ricard%2C%2069%2C%20is%20a,University%20of%20Wisconsin%2C%20Richard%20Davidson, accessed 27 June 2023.

[7] Impact can be anything from satisfied customers to increased profits to improved living conditions.

[8] Illustration by the author inspired by contents in Trost, A. (2013). *Employer Branding: Arbeitgeber positionieren und präsentieren*. Cologne: Luchterhand.

Chapter 4 The process of recruiting the best team

[1] Trost, A. (2014). *Talent Relationship Management: Competitive Recruiting Strategies in Times of Talent Shortage*. Berlin/Heidelberg: Springer, p. 41.

[2] Inspired by a quote by Carl W. Buechner in Evans, R. (1971), *Richard Evans' Quote Book*. Salt Lake City: Publishers Press, p. 244.

[3] Active candidates are those who are actively looking for jobs and are actively reading ads on different platforms, channels, and professional or social media. Passive candidates are those who are not actively searching, but may be triggered by an appropriate outreach or message to consider and review certain job opportunities. Non-candidates are those who are so happy in their current job and company that they cannot be triggered by an outreach. "Non-candidates" is what companies want to achieve with their best people—that they are non-candidates because they are perfectly happy where they are.

[4] The bias a machine applies, or doesn't apply, ultimately depends on the human who programmed it.

[5] MIT Career Advising & Professional Development (n.d.). Using the STAR method for your next behavioral interview. https://capd.mit.edu/resources/the-star-method-for-behavioral-interviews/, accessed 6 September 2024.

[6] "There can be only one" is the belief and motto of the Immortals in the original *Highlander* movie as well as in its sequels and spin-offs. It implies that all the Immortals must fight and kill each other until only one is left standing; that "one" will receive the prize.

Chapter 5 The role of technology: How AI can help you recruit the best team

[1] But keep in mind that AI cannot eliminate bias. Since it is created by humans, some level of bias is inherently built into the system.

[2] Jakesch, M. (2023). Human heuristics for AI-generated language are flawed. https://www.pnas.org/doi/10.1073/pnas.2208839120, accessed 4 December 2023.

[3] Handler, C. (2023). I interviewed ChatGPT about the future and hiring and the results are profound and hilarious. https://www.spreaker.com/episode/i-interviewed-chatgpt-about-the-future-of-hiring-and-the-results-are-profound-and-hilarious--57567217, accessed 4 December 2023.

Chapter 6 Recruitment is more than recruitment

[1] Jung, C., & Desikan, B. S. (2024). *Transformed by AI: How Generative Artificial Intelligence Could Affect Work in the UK—and How to Manage It*. London: Institute for Public Policy Research, p. 23.

Index

A

AI *see artificial intelligence*
Ambler, Tim 28
artificial intelligence 91–104
    in the individual steps of the recruitment process 99
assessing candidates 84
"aura" of an employer 30
automation 104–105
autonomy 54–55, 58–59, 60–61

B

Barrow, Simon 28
beliefs about your role as a recruiter 9
buying and selling approach to recruitment 12
buying a team or company 109

C

certain something 28, 35
    how to find it 30, 36
ChatGPT 94–95, 97
Churchill, Winston 3
coaching 17
collaboration 108
core values 31–32, 37
creating a need 67, 99
curiosity 22

D

deciding for a candidate 100
describing the job 67
development- and growth-oriented candidate 20
Dweck, Carol 25

E

empathy 22
employer branding 28
ESG 51–52
ethos 51, 58–61

F

Filler, Ellie 15
freelancers 106

G

"glass is half empty" mindset 10
"glass is half full" mindset 11
GLOBE study 51

H

Hawthorne experiments 25
honesty 21, 51, 61
Houston, Melissa 26
HR business partner 14

I

impact 56
"inside-out" approach 47–48, 59, 62
inspiration 52, 58
integrity 51, 58
interviewing candidates 81, 100 *see also job interview*
investment 23

J

Jacobson, Lenore F. 25
job advertisement 74
job description 67

job interview 81–82, 84
job requirements 69–70

L

leadership 19–20
learning 57
LinkedIn 30, 42, 75, 77, 94–96, 115
logos 53–54, 58

M

magic moments 70, 72–73
mastery 57–58, 60–61
matching process 8
mindset 5
money-oriented candidate 20
Musk, Elon 19

N

negotiating with candidates 87, 100
net problem 24
NXP 1
Nyad, Diana 3

O

onboarding 89–90, 101
"outside-in" view of HR management 47–49
outsourcing 108

P

pathos 52, 58, 60
Philips 1
process of recruiting 65–66, 90
promoting the job 74
purchasing process 13
purpose 31, 34, 39, 56, 58, 60–61

R

recruiting friends 7–8
recruitment
    as buying and selling 12, 16
    as investment 23, 26
    as leading and coaching 17
    mindset 5, 12
    process 65–66, 90
rejecting applicants 85
résumés 100
Rosenthal, Robert 25

S

sales process 13
screening candidates 76, 80
screening résumés 100
shriveled apple 27
Sinek, Simon 18
six key elements of a story 51
Snigel 32, 36, 37–39, 59, 61
solution orientation 22
STARL method 83
story 27, 41, 47
    authentic "core" 59
    making an impact 58
    matching it with requirements of stakeholder groups 61
    six key elements 51
    who to tell it to 42, 43–44

T

temporary staff 105
testing candidates 81
Trost, Armin 70
trust 26
trustworthiness 51, 58
types of problems 24

U

Ulrich, Dave 14–15, 48–49
uniqueness as an employer 31, 40
upskilling your team 107

W

Winterheller, Manfred 24

About the author

Dr. Barbara Stampf is an internationally active recruiter, coach, and business angel. Formerly a human resources manager at leading global companies (Philips, NXP), she now runs her own business development and recruitment agency, helping technology companies attract talent, investors, and customers during their growth phase. Barbara is also a venture partner at Cloudberry Investment Pioneers (*cpi.vc*), a venture capital firm that invests in the areas of renewable energy, semiconductors, computing, and fintech. Her mission is to empower people to be happier, stronger, and more successful.

Work with us in business development & executive search

Develop your business & your people

Together with our partners at PKF Business Development GmbH, we help you grow your business on a global scale. We work with you to develop a compelling strategy and a story that attracts strategic investors and buyers, business partners, and top talent. We assess, develop and recruit your top team. Our focus lies on technology companies with an international reach.

Recruitment & executive search

We take on your strategic executive search tasks. We analyse your business, the job, the competitive landscape, and your employer attractiveness. We craft a compelling story for the job market. We search, find and select candidates with you and for you. We coach and mentor candidates with passion, from the first interview to onboarding.

Training, coaching & speaking engagements

Book Barbara for an inspirational speech on how to recruit the best team. Our services also include one-on-one coaching and customized training programs for your leadership team in the field of recruitment.

Contact Barbara directly via email at *office@barbara-stampf.at*

Boost your confidence, inspire others, become a better leader!

Whether you are new to a leadership role or want to take your existing leadership competencies to a higher level—here's the most practical guide for you. With **50 skill-building exercises** that will help you grow as a leader right away … and with heartwarming illustrations that will allow you to 'feel' what effective leadership really means.

Develop Your Leadership Superpowers: 50 Key Skills You Need to Succeed as a Leader by Dietmar Sternad and Eva Kobin is available wherever good books and ebooks are sold.

Printed in Dunstable, United Kingdom